CONTEN

C000053269

ABOUT THE AUTHOR

B ro Neville Barker Cryer was educated at Manchester Grammar School and Oxford, where his studies were interrupted between 1942 and 1946 by military service with the Indian Army. In 1948/49, after completing his degree in history, he studied theology at Cambridge, being ordained in 1950. His first curacy was in Derby, followed by Ilkeston. He was initiated into the Mother Lodge of Derbyshire, Tyrian Lodge No 253, in December 1950. He is still a member and is now the longest serving member on the roll. He late joined Wolseley Lodge No 1993 and was exalted in 1956 in Affability Chapter No 317, both at Bridge Street, Manchester. In 1960 he became vicar of a parish in East Croydon and was soon to become one of the founders, and Junior Warden, of Comet Lodge No 7710. Over the past 55 years Bro Cryer has held many positions of note within Freemasonry; these include, in 1974, being the Prestonian Lecturer (Grand Chaplain 1986-88) and, in 1996–98, the Batham Lecturer. It is with pride that he became the first English Freemason to have held both official lecturer appointments. He has also been the W.M., Secretary and Editor of the Quatuor Coronati Lodge No 2076 and has been W.M. of the Manchester Lodge of Masonic Research, No 5502. Outside Freemasonry, Bro Cryer became Home Secretary of the Conference of British Missionary Societies in October 1967. In 1970 he became the General Secretary — later General Director — of the British & Foreign Bible Society, a post from which he retired in 1986. Twice married and now resident in York, Bro Cryer continues his active involvement in Freemasonry as he looks forward to the 60th anniversary of membership of the Craft.

Did You Know This, Too?

Revd Neville Barker Cryer

For Frank

warm regards

Neville Barker

Cryer

Lewis  Masonic

First published 2005
This impression 2008

ISBN 978 0 85318 241 2

Published by Lewis Masonic

an imprint of Ian Allan Publishing Ltd, Hersham, Surrey
KT12 4RG.
Printed in England by Ian Allan Printing Ltd, Hersham,
Surrey KT12 4RG.

By the same author.
What Do You Know About The Royal Arch?
(ISBN 978 0 85318 227 2)

I Just Didn't Know That
(ISBN 978 0 85318 219 1)

Visit the Lewis Masonic web site at:
www.lewismasonic.com

THE CHURCHES' INVOLVEMENT WITH FREEMASONRY

The idea for this lecture first came to me some years ago when the Craft in England had been subjected to some fairly heavy criticism from first the Methodist Church and then the Church of England. As half my ancestry, that on my father's side, has been staunch Methodist and my mother's family derived from a priest at the Reformation, who could at last marry as a cleric of the Church of England, I felt the attacks with some force. It seemed to me, as one who had been ordained to the ministry of the Anglican Church in Derby Cathedral and initiated in Tyrian Lodge in Derby in the same year, to be manifestly ridiculous to admit that it was impossible to be both a good churchman and a regular Mason. I knew from a lifetime of involvement in both that it was entirely compatible for one to have deep faith and sincere Masonic commitment.

I wrote a paper called 'Faith and Freemasonry' to make the point, just as I had also written a paper called 'The Churches' concern with Freemasonry' to outline the history of how we had arrived at this sad situation. Yet I felt that there was another side to this whole story that was not being told. A chance word with another Past Grand Chaplain, Canon Richard Tydeman, then the recently appointed Most Puissant Sovereign Grand Commander of the Supreme Council 33°, confirmed me in my view. He felt, as I do, that what was being overlooked was the very long-standing involvement of churchmen and church fabric in Freemasonry and the very rich mine of material that there was available to prove the point. 'Why don't you write about that?' he said. I told him that I had already begun to do so. This lecture is the first fruits of that common conviction.

I must begin with a bit more autobiography. It was a few months after my ordination that I attended a Diocesan Conference at Matlock Bath. As I left the morning session I was called to one side by a gaitered and aproned cleric, the Venerable Henry Edward Fitzherbert, Archdeacon of Derby. His family is of the same lineage as the second husband of the morganatic wife of George IV. His first question was rather odd.

'Have you a good memory, young man?' he asked.

'Fairly good,' I replied, to which he responded by inviting me to tea at his Vicarage the following Sunday.

All agog to learn what was afoot, I turned up at the Old Rectory and was served tea on the lawn. His wife withdrew and from an inside pocket the Archdeacon took a large piece of printed paper.

'This is something I want you to sign,' he declared.

'What is it?' I asked, having had some experience of forms in the Army.

'It is your entry form into Freemasonry and we want you in. Your seconder is Canon Boorman at the Cathedral and he is pleased to support you.'

As I had never even heard of Freemasonry until that moment it was all a surprise, and yet what was my impression? Here was a senior Church officer, backed up by the Diocesan Secretary, eager to arrange part of my future. For them there was not the slightest problem about the twin membership of Church and Craft and indeed it looked as if the step into Masonry was one which local Church leaders not only approved of but actively promoted. I signed up.

The connection with the Church seemed stronger than ever when I at last 'came to light' in the lodge temple. There, amongst the surrounding faces, I saw the Director of Diocesan Education, another Canon; the chief lecturer at the Diocesan Training College for Lady Teachers, the Rev Dr Daines; there were two other incumbents, and a visiting cleric, Canon John Richardson, who was in due course to become the Archdeacon of Derby, following my proposer. Is it any wonder that I came into the Craft with the firm conviction that the Church was indeed very closely linked with our Order? Oh, and I forgot to say that amongst the laymen present was one of the churchwardens of the parish church in which I was serving as a curate, along with a lawyer who was later to become the Diocesan Registrar. Just to put the lid on firmly, I received from a cousin shortly afterwards a note saying that she was glad to know that I was a Freemason. Her dad, my dear uncle George Bailey, a senior steward of Bank Street Methodist church in Hadfield, Derbyshire, had apparently been a Provincial officer. I hope that you now see why I grew up with the unquestioned belief that the Churches were inevitably linked with Freemasonry.

Since then I have had many similar examples of such close ties. One of our Quatuor Coronati Lodge's most regular attenders as a Correspondence Circle member was the 82-year-old Provincial Archivist for Hampshire. Entering his local lodge at the age of 24 he found that, besides his proposer, the Baptist church Bible class leader, and his seconder, the Senior Deacon of the church, there were the Baptist minister, the Sunday School head, two more Deacons and one of the church's foremost supporters. Imagine his amazement a few years ago when a new Baptist minister, fresh out of college, told him that unless he gave up his devilish practices as a Mason he would be barred from membership, after nearly 70 years of regular attendance.

As I began to get my own bearings and learn about the words, customs and history of this 'Society of Masons' to which I belonged, the connection with the Church became more and more evident. Not only was the Established Church's Authorised Version of the Scriptures appointed to be open in all the lodges I attended, but also it was a cleric of the Established Church in Scotland, Dr James Anderson, who was chosen to be the author of the first *Constitutions* by which this new growth of Freemasonry was to be regulated. Even more, a member of the Huguenot Church exiled to England, Dr John Desaguliers, was one of the first Grand Masters and so involved were the members of that religious community in this new body that many of the early Grand Officers are clearly recognisable as from that group. The Huguenot Lodge in London invited me to write a paper, on the phenomenon of such close association, for the 300th Anniversary of the Huguenot community in England some years ago and it was accepted as a subject for printing in their Society journal.

What was soon evident in the practice of private lodges up and down the land was the custom of a lodge processing to or gathering at the local parish church before the important occasion of Installation and the hearing of a sermon with prayers conducted either by the parson or the chaplain of the lodge — sometimes, of course, being the same person. Nor were these occasions without their opportunity for contributing either to the needs of the church attended or to some nearby charitable work which had the church's approval. As but one example at random, let me introduce you to the lodge at Barton-upon-Humber, not the most readily identifiable town in the United Kingdom. What follows was unearthed when I included the Masonic Hall in my book about the buildings in the northern part of England.

'On 14 August 1816 the Revd. George Oliver, Vicar of Clee, P.M. of the Apollo Lodge No. 544 of Great Grimsby, and Provincial Grand Chaplain of the Province of Lincoln, preached a sermon at St. Peter's Church as part of the Provincial Meeting of the United Grand Lodge.' So runs a passage from a booklet about the occasion which, with the text of the sermon, is still preserved in the hall at Barton. The sermon includes the following: 'The Secrets of this truly valuable Art are of a nature so consonant with the mysteries of Christianity that whoever is possessed of the sublimities of the former cannot be deficient in the practice of the latter . . .' and he added in a footnote, 'It has ever been my religion; those we derive from Eden, from the patriarchs, and from the sages of the East, all of which are made perfect under the Christian dispensation', and that is not all that that lodge room reveals.

Let us move to another part of the country altogether. In 1985 I was in Poole, Dorset, to give a lecture. After the festive board a Past Master asked me if, before I went away the next morning, I would like to be shown round the parish church of St James close by. He was one of the churchwardens and was rightly proud of the ancient building. I agreed and was indeed impressed with the beautiful condition of the fabric and the charming 18th-century style of its interior. The brother especially led my eye to a number of fine wall plaques commemorating various men of note in the parish. There was also one panel for a notable lady.

When we had made the tour, the warden told me the following story. A new Vicar had come to Poole about six months or so previously and shortly after his arrival he found occasion to make a plain but somewhat ill-informed attack upon the prevalence of Freemasonry that had come to his notice whilst visiting the congregation in their homes. He concluded by hoping — or rather praying — that those who followed this way would soon be led to recognise their errors and let their Church faith have sole sway. My companion had a word with his fellow churchwarden, who was also a Mason, and they asked the Vicar to meet them one evening in the church building. The Vicar, a trifle mystified at this request, turned up and was taken on the same tour as myself. This time, however, he was informed that more than three-quarters of the persons mentioned in the plaques had been Freemasons, including the son of the lady whose panel is there.

'Without them,' said the Mason-wardens, 'this church and its influence in society hereabouts would have been very considerably reduced. Perhaps, Vicar, you should consider in future those amongst whom you are preaching.' It had, I was told, a rather chastening effect.

This story is paralleled in the present day by the complaint of the Vicar of Hampton who not long ago remarked to his curate, who was a Mason, that the Charity Garden Party for Masons the previous afternoon seemed to have depleted the attendance at the 8 am Sunday service. Respectfully the curate pointed out that the only men in the congregation that morning were Masons.

The mention of church fabric must surely lead us into the whole area of Masonic adornment of churches. Three years ago I had the sad duty of attending the funeral of the best man at my marriage, himself also a cleric and one with whom I shared my theological college days. He had spent his short retirement helping in the beautiful parish of Clare in Suffolk until he died with a crippling cancer.

As I sat in the large parish church pondering the life of my friend, my eyes were drawn to a huge Decorated-style side window which contained lovely stained glass portraying the story of the good Samaritan. Far up the road were the figures of the Priest and the Levite and in the foreground was the Samaritan tending the wounds of the mugged Hebrew traveller, whilst a patient ass waited to receive its burden and carry him to the nearest inn. The care which my friend had shown amongst Italian prisoners of war as their Commandant in North Africa, as a curate in the East End of London, and as the parson in a large country parish near Chelmsford — all seemed to be summed up in that picture.

When the service was over and we had seen his body laid to rest, I went back into the church and stood under the window again. What did I read at the foot of the glass panels? 'This window was given to the glory of God and in loving and fraternal affection and memory of the Revd. Canon [and then his name], Deputy Provincial Grand Master of this Province for 15 years, by the brethren of Suffolk.' I later discovered that not only had the Canon been sometime Vicar of this parish but also that it was here that he too ended his days. It was yet one more moving connection between the Church and Freemasonry and the beauty of that gift will be an ongoing inspiration as long as that building stands.

Examples of Masonic contributions for the enhancement of church buildings are so numerous that it is well-nigh impossible to know where to begin and to end. Whether it be the organ casing of the largest parish church in England at Great Yarmouth — duly inscribed as a Masonic gift for all to see — or whether it be the exquisite ironwork over the pilgrim chapel entrance and the huge west window in the Cathedral of Guildford, Surrey, the same message is still being proclaimed.

What the Church of the Middle Ages owed to the operative masons who carved the great vaults and raised the vast walls is symbolised by the Apprentice Pillar in Rosslyn Chapel near Edinburgh, whilst the Church today still owes much to the speculative Masons who seek to provide ornaments of quality that do honour and give glory to God's house and name. A symbol of this latter is the Masons' Pillar in the present Anglican Cathedral in Belfast, Northern Ireland. I forbear to stress the willingness of those having huge cathedral repair bills to accept the many gifts made by our Grand Charity — like the recent contribution made to restock the tools and improve the conditions in the Masons' Yard at York. Every time that sort of thing happens the link between the Church and the Craft is renewed — not begun — and the point I am trying to illustrate in this paper is made once more.

Finally, for this evening, I want us to move out of the church building into the churchyard that surrounds it. This area, called in the past 'God's Acre', has always been regarded as of special importance to the Church community and has been regulated with particular care. Even to the present day there are occasional newspaper items when a family is apparently in conflict with the local parish priest or church council about what can and what cannot be allowed in these hallowed precincts. I mention this requirement because it makes the appearance of memorial stones with Masonic emblems all the more significant. Clearly the Church in the past had no hang-ups about the inclusion of Masonic burials in the church's own cemetery.

That this is not just a fanciful notion seems to be supported by the view of a previous Librarian of Grand Lodge, Henry Sadler, who contended that in 1717 Freemasonry was still largely a trade-orientated society and that a struggle for control took place in the 1720s between *the original operative members* and those brought into the lodges under the influence of Dr Desaguliers, a close associate of Anderson's.

It may at first seem somewhat odd that in a paper which suggests the *contribution* of operative to speculative Masonry I should so early refer to what looks like a case of exclusion. That may be the impression but I would ask you to be patient and to consider some other facts in that important period before jumping to any conclusion. For I would next draw to your attention the subject on which Thomas Carr further wrote: 'The Ritual of the Operative Masons'.

There are those, of course, who hold that the Primitive Operative Craft ritual was of such a simple, bald, unattractive, or even commonplace character that it was quite incapable of providing any pattern for the developing forms of the early 18th century. An opposing view is that those who object to the claim of the Operative Free Masons, that they were always divided into *seven* grades, on the ground that that is *too elaborate a division* and suggests *too involved a ritual* for the ancient masons to have invented, are using 'an argument too futile for words'.

Just consider, continues this latter view, who these ancient masons were and what buildings they erected. These were the men who built our cathedrals and churches, hundreds of which still stand to testify to their skill and that of the bishops, abbots and priests who were associated with these masons and were themselves often the architects. That anyone should dare to suggest that such men as these could not invent or, as is more likely, perpetuate and develop a system such as the present-day Operative Free Masons practise, is incredible to anyone who knows the work these men did and the manner of men they were.

Despite the apparent contrast between these two points of view Bro Gould is on record as saying that 'the importance of the Mark Degree as a connecting link with the operative masons' *customs and traditions* prior to the formation of the premier Grand Lodge is not always fully appreciated, particularly by (English) Freemasons'. Perhaps Gould has here pointed us to the missing factor in our search for origins. He speaks of 'customs and traditions' *rather than degree ceremonies*, suggesting not that we can derive from some ancient ritual texts a form of ceremony such as we are accustomed to today but that, lying in wait to be so employed in Speculative Freemasonry, there were long-standing forms of instruction as well as customary practices that could be so shaped. Eric Ward, another distinguished scholar Freemason, wrote in 1962 of a realisation amongst Masons that 'material once possessing infinite mystical value had somehow been discarded [and] was capable of revival and expansion into a rite *purporting to restore* the genuine secrets'. He also went on: 'One of the peculiarities of ritual growth is that customs *discarded in one place turn up surprisingly in another* at a much later date.' That is a profound insight into the development of Speculative Masonic practice that deserves much more comment but which again cannot be pursued here.

The Operative Free Masons, I contend, retained enough tradition that by the second quarter of the 18th century they also had their own catechisms, lectures and rituals which embraced the legends, customs and practices from which the Speculative Masons adapted their own more restricted models. We now have access in the North-East of England to lecture material from about 1740 which illustrates just such a claim.

For those who know nothing of the past in this connection it should be noted that a Guild of Operative Free Masons flourished in England until about 1870. It then diminished owing to altered economic conditions and the growing influence of the Trade Unions. By the time of the First World War there were only a few of its lodges existing and it was from a lodge of over 300 members at Bardon in Leicestershire that there came that same Thomas Carr whose work we have already encountered. He was greatly helped in his presentation by Clement Stretton, who was a senior member of the Leicestershire operatives, and it was his copy of the ritual which was eventually presented to myself by a Past Third Grand Master of the present Speculative Order of Operatives who had himself held it for much of his lifetime. It was only in preparing my recent book that the full significance of what I possessed suddenly began to dawn upon me.

The full title of the originally operative body with which we are here concerned was 'The Worshipful Society of Free Masons, Rough Masons, Wallers, Slaters, Paviors, Plaisterers and Bricklayers'. And it is in the City of Durham that we find exactly the same trades combined as in the overall parent Society.

In 1594 the Prince Bishop of Durham, Matthew Hutton, had incorporated the Rough Masons, Wallers and Slaters, whilst in 1609 Bishop William James confirmed the bylaws and ordinances of a body that had added Paviors, Tylers and Plaisterers. Finally, on 16 April 1638, Bishop Thomas Morton, acting in his capacity as a Count Palatine, gave a new charter to 'The Company, Societie and the Fellowshipp of Free Masons Rough Masons Wallers Slaytors Pavers Plaisterers and Bricklayers'. These operatives became Freemen of the City of Durham and many of the gentry of the County became Honorary Members of the Company, regarding it as an honourable distinction. The same is still true of professional and business men joining the Honourable or Livery Companies in the City of London to this day.

In the year 1677 'The Worshipful Society of the Free Masons of the City of London' (note: *not* the Company) issued a map of England on which was shown the division of the operatives into eight districts:

1. City of London
2. Westminster
3. Southern
4. Bristol
5. Chester
6. Island of Anglesea [*sic*]
7. Lancaster
8. York

These divisions are of singular interest to the Masonic student as they indicate the areas in or through which antient Masonry later developed.

From their earliest period of existence the operative masons were divided into two classes: Straight or Square Masons, and Round or Arch Masons. The reason for this was that the straight work needed less skill, and hence was able to command less wages, than

20

the art of making arches, bridges and all kinds of curved, carved or graved work. The two classes were each divided into seven grades:

Apprentice to the Craft of Free Mason.
Fellow of the Craft of Free Mason.
Super Fellow, who had his mark.
Super Fellow Erector, who worked on the stone.
Super-Intendent of the Craft, or *Menatzchim*.
Passed Master of the Craft, who had literally 'passed a technical examination' to attain the position of a Master, as Masters of sailing vessels still have to qualify. He was thus a properly certificated Master who was also known, especially in the North-East of England, as a *Harod* (plural: *Harodim*).
Master Mason, or Grand Master of the Craft of Free Masons.

The traditional reason given why the operative Free Masons need to be thus graded was because when Solomon began to build the temple on Mount Moriah he needed specific persons for its different stages and tasks. Thus he could ensure that 'the house shall be built of stone made ready before it was brought hither: so that there shall be neither hammer nor axe nor any tool of iron heard in the house while it was in building'. That required careful planning and strict administration to ensure that every stone was made to a required size and gauge in the second degree stone-yard. It was then fitted and marked by the Mark Men in the third degree yard so that the erectors on the actual building site could quietly set each stone in its indicated place. Anyone who has wondered where the idea of the *Silent Temple* came from can now appreciate its operative source.

A man was allowed to belong to only one of the two classes (i.e. the Square or the Arch Masons) but he was allowed to transfer from one to the other if the Masters so ordered it. When a young man was apprenticed, at the age of 14 after 1663, though previously it had been at 12 or 13, he chose in which class he wished to serve. Whilst the Craft after 1717 gives the impression of restricting entry merely to 'squaremen', it is worth noting that Arch work was known and might thus be involved later.

It is also to be noted that an apprentice was not regarded as being a member of the Craft. Indeed a General Assembly was held by the operative rulers in Wakefield on 8 December 1663, where they agreed that no person should be accepted a Free Mason until he was 21 years of age. You do not need me to remind you that to this day the Craft in the USA does not accept an apprentice as a full member of the lodge. Here again we have the direct influence of operative practice, just as we do in the way that Scottish and Irish Masons wear the apron under and not over their jackets. If the young man decided to be a Straight Mason he was given a square and if an Arch Mason the compasses. If, therefore, you might want to find a hostelry where both classes of working masons would congregate, you looked for an inn with the sign of the Square and Compasses. The very combination of these implements in present Freemasonry reveals that materials and customs from both classes were adapted in order to form the new practices after 1717.

The ultimate secrets (which were more than handshakes) and the whole ritual of the operative 'Masters' could not be given, as but few knew them: namely, only those who

21

had actually been one of the three Grand Masters (Seventh Degree) by whom the operatives were ruled, and though Dr Anderson was once a Chaplain in an Accepted Lodge *he was not privy to all its secrets*. Even so we do have an interesting, and for some a still puzzling, feature. In the first 15 years of the Premier Grand Lodge we note a regulation stating that no one might adopt the grade of 'Master' of a lodge until he had received a certain ceremony in the Grand Lodge when three Grand Officers, themselves ruling Masters, were in the principal chairs. When you know the operative practice you at last understand why, but to grasp the full implications of this practice needs another lecture.

The three operative Grand Masters were, of course, the same for both Square and Arch Masonry and hence their non-involvement elsewhere, in any plans for the new type of Craft Masonry, meant that much was left out that would have helped to explain the omissions that were soon noticed by older operative members. This, and Irish tradition (and that is a subject needing a lecture all on its own), is what helped in the formation of Arch Masonry (another neglected topic) and subsequently the practices of the Antients from the 1750s. Yet why was Desaguliers holding a lodge (or was it chapter?) of Super-excellent Masons as early as 1735?

The colour of the Square Mason was blue, whilst the Arch Mason was distinguished by red. A lot of time and ingenuity in discussing the origin and appropriateness of Masonic colours could have been saved if only this traditional fact were better known. These colours are clearly illustrated if one examines the original Arms of the Society of the Free Masons granted by Edward IV and which eventually had two supporters. The one on the right side was a mason with a *square* in his hand and with *blue* facings on his jacket, whilst the figure balancing him on the other side is an Arch mason with, yes, *red* facings and holding a *pair of compasses*.

The operatives at work

The lodge room for the operatives' working up to the old Fifth Degree was orientated so that the Masters were in the *West* in order to *face* the rising sun. The Junior Warden sat in the *North* to *see* the sun at its meridian, and the Senior Warden sat in the *East* so as to *observe* the setting sun. This was the same orientation as of the Holy Place in the temple at Jerusalem and it also explains why the Antient Freemasons insisted on this type of lodge formation for the principal officers in the initial degrees.

When you learn that in the higher operative degrees the officers sat either with the Right Worshipful Master at one end and the Wardens facing him at the other or that the Grand Masters sat side by side, then you begin to grasp why we adopt the former in the Ark Mariner degree and the latter in the Holy Royal Arch.

The altar was in the centre of the lodge (another Scottish, Irish and American custom, still) and there were three Deacons, the Master also being so served. There are still Craft Lodges in England where there are vestiges of the three Deacons.

The entry of the *Apprentice* in such a lodge is to be noted. He was hoodwinked, clothed in a white cloak, but he also had a blue cord around his middle, the ends held taut by two brethren, one on each side. In addition, one man in front and one behind held the ends of another blue cord around his neck. Here we have the origins of a cable tow about the neck but also the Antients' use of the cord about the middle to signify our being

22

qualified Masons. Thus was also formed *a diamond of five points* which had not only operative but subsequent Mark significance.

When asked how he hoped to obtain admission, he claimed the help of El Shaddai (a term not restricted to the Royal Arch) and used another phrase familiar to us in this context, which is actually the password of the First Degree. When he came to his obligation he knelt at the central altar, which had a rough ashlar to the east of it, and placed his left hand flat under the Volume of the Sacred Law whilst laying his right hand flat upon it. This is, of course, still preserved in lodges under the Grand Lodge of Scotland as the 'due guard' sign.

The candidate then took an obligation which remained the same from when it was first written out and signed by Robert Padgett, Clerk to the Worshipful Society of Free Masons of London in 1686. One copy is supposed to have been taken by Dr Anderson but is now in the possession of the Lodge of Antiquity. A similar oath is found in the *Kilwinning MS No 4*, which only serves to emphasise its antiquity. Once again we see the provenance of Grand Lodge practice in operative custom.

Moving on to the *Fellow of the Craft* degree, the candidate had to prepare a rough-dressed ashlar as a specimen of his work and the Inspector of Materials had to pass it before he could proceed. He also *had to have this specimen with him* when he entered the lodge and had to declare that it was all his own work. He was obligated, given the sign with the right hand flat, and the word *Banai*, meaning 'Builder'. If we wonder where the substituted word of the 3° came from, we are here given a clue.

The Charge that was delivered was one that was also produced by Robert Padgett in 1686 and signed by him for use in all the eight divisions of the country. Two of its provisions are noteworthy:

(1) You shall honour El Shaddai and his Holy Church: that you use no Heresy, Schism nor Error in your Undertakings, or discredit wise Men's teachings.
(4) You shall keep Secret the obscure and *intricate Parts* of the Science, not disclosing them to any but such as *study* and use the same. [We all know what is the present object of the Fellow of the Craft degree.]

The candidate then received the sign and word as above but in addition to the usual tools he was also given another straight edge, the two-foot rule, and the perfect Ashlar Square. The latter was a wooden frame with overlapping corners which was the exact size of a Royal Cubit. He was then a Free Man and a Free Mason and was directed to begin work in the north-east corner of the yard where he was required to make his rough dressed Ashlar into a stone true and polished. Do you again wonder where the origin of the north-east charge and practice began?

When completed, his work had to be submitted for inspection and tried so that, if satisfactory, he might receive a word, *Giblim*, which meant 'stone squarer' or 'expert mason'. Interestingly, the words of this operative degree suggest how the adaptation and rearrangement took place after 1717. It is known that Dr Anderson was aware of these words because he mentions them in the 1738 edition of the *Book of Constitutions* but because, as we have noted, he had an imperfect knowledge of their place and use he and/or others used them differently.

23

The mason having made his test piece, he had it approved by the Inspector of Materials and, having served another year as a Fellow, he was then eligible to apply for the degree of Super Fellow. Notice having been given by a form posted in the yard, and the sign, word and work having been presented, the candidate entered into what the speculative Mark Mason of today would recognise as the degree of Mark Man. The Super Fellow was allotted his Mark and charged to produce 'fare work and square'. He was led round the lodge three times and took his obligation kneeling on his bare knees and *on the polished stone* he brought with him.

His next step was that of Erector and here we discover that an interesting distinction occurred. The stone that was found to be missing amongst Square masons was the *chief cornerstone*, whilst among the Arch masons it was the *keystone*. The moral that was pointed up was the same in both ceremonies. We again have the origin of the Craft Mason standing at the north-east corner, whilst for the English Royal Arch Mason we have the solution of what seems in our present working a surprising new feature, the keystone, that is never clearly explained.

The candidate took his obligation, this time kneeling on a perfect polished stone, was led *four* times round the lodge and the word and sign given were those of the degree today. If one again wonders why in a few very old chapters in England the candidate is led four times round the chapter room before he approaches the keystone we are again enlightened. This was as far as most operative masons ever went, since considerable technical knowledge was required before proceeding further. What is to be noted is that every operative mason did have all the *Mark* knowledge that awaits us today. If there are those in speculative Freemasonry who wonder at those, as in the York Rite, who claim a place for the Mark in the Masonic scheme it is because that was the natural development in the old craft. There were also in the remaining operative customs some features that we need to take note of. The term 'Superintendent' came from their Fifth Degree, thus showing its subordinate status to that of the Grand Master in the Arch class, whilst for Mark Masons the word of the degree, *Menatzchim*, has a more familiar ring.

The 'Passed Master' or Sixth Degree required that a candidate should be able to '*lay schemes, draw plans*, and take charge of a department'. With this step, which was equivalent to that of a present reigning Master, it can be understood why the Antients insisted that here one had a *separate* and *essential* degree before moving on to Arch Masonry. Moreover, the senior Passed Master was called 'Adoniram' and the word of this degree was *Harod* or *Harodim*. From the limited lodge of 15 members in this grade, *three members only* were able to proceed to the long-serving degree of Grand Master. They were led round the lodge room seven times and, according to the class they were in, they represented either the Craft Grand Masters, Solomon, Hiram, and Hiram Abif, or the Three Principals as we know them in a Royal Arch chapter today (except in Ireland).

In the lodge room a new arrangement was then adopted with the three Grand Masters sitting together in the west but at the top of seven steps. Here is also the reason why seven steps are provided in some old lodge rooms in England for the Worshipful Master's Chair. Below the steps sat Adoniram and in the east were the two pillars with Passed Masters behind them, facing west. Boaz was on the left facing east, and Jachin on the right, and that should help anyone who wonders which is the correct placing of the great pillars.

Scotland? Why, moreover, does any English Freemasonry of the 17th century suddenly appear as if it had come from nowhere, with no obvious operative connections, with a preponderance of genteel, professional or other trade members, and meeting in what are recognisable lodges? How can this apparently *ad hoc* attachment to a movement called Freemasonry be recognised by such a non-Masonic commentator as Dr Plot as an organisation that appears to spread across the nation?

What, moreover, are we to make of even Dr Stevenson's admission that 'whereas freemasonry began in Scotland with the foundation of lodges around 1600, in England it began with individual initiates, sometimes deriving their ritual and secrets from English operative masons'? Where did that information come from? What do we make of his further statement that 'whereas most Scottish lodges long retained close links with working stonemasons, who usually indeed still formed a majority of members . . . the English lodges were founded by gentlemen enthusiasts who felt little or no need to seek legitimacy by developing links with "real" stonemasons'? (*The First Freemasons*, p. 160)

It is when we make an attempt to grapple with these remaining, and yet essential, questions that we can perhaps begin to discern some of the features that suggest a different origin for Freemasonry in England as compared with Scotland.

That Scotland's experience and understanding in these matters did have some influence on how English Freemasons conceived the Craft may be admitted. Interestingly, even Stevenson admits that this was at *the end* of the 17th century and not at its beginning. There is clearly no time or space in this presentation to reflect adequately on the attitude of Englishmen to the Scots from the time of Mary, Queen of Scots, to the later Stuarts. Even James VI of the Northern Kingdom had to become James I of England and, cautious as he was in preserving his dual crown, he knew that little love was lost between his separate subjects. Charles I was inept in his treatment of his Scottish subjects and the Civil War in England did little to endear the two nations, despite some Protestant similarities.

It is in this fraught context that we have to put the initiation of Moray at Newcastle and recognise that whatever the Scots might do in such a case was unlikely to be accepted automatically as a guide by English brethren. The restoration of episcopacy and even pro-Romanism under the Stuart Restoration did nothing to improve national relations, whilst the despatch of the Stuart line from 1688 started a fear of Scottish reaction which was to last until the middle of the next century. To pretend, along with appallingly bad roads, that communication with Scotland was constant and influential is to misunderstand the circumstances of the time. In the 18th century anything beyond York was thought of as 'Northern Britain' and that included the whole of Scotland. It was not until a Union of the two countries was imminent, or created, that real interchange of ideas and culture was developed. Desaguliers' visit to Edinburgh makes the point, whilst Dr Johnson's visit with Boswell was to cement it.

What we have to face up to is the point well made by John Hamill in his book *The Craft*. Speaking of the 'authentic school' of researchers like Harry Carr, he says: 'Above all they overlooked, or ignored, the fact that non-operative masonry was developing in England when the Scottish operative lodges began to accept non-operatives. If the Scottish operative lodges formed the medium of transition, how could purely non-operative masonry already have existed in England?' (*The Craft*, p. 19)

29

Perhaps the most significant difference to be noted as between early English and Scottish Freemasonry is that whilst it is clear that there were continuing and established operative lodges in Scotland, the 17th century saw the emergence in England of *ad hoc* or temporary lodges which met only for as long as their occasion for meeting existed.

Once we accept that this is a major point of difference then we can begin to account for several pieces of evidence in 17th-century England that seem otherwise disconnected and confusing. We can appreciate why there are disparate dates for Freemasons visiting and existing in York. We can appreciate why Ashmole speaks of attending a lodge at Warrington which seems to be a 'one-off' occasion. We have evidence of a lodge in Chester though it does not meet regularly. We have the 'Acception' lodge connected with the Company of Masons in London which also met irregularly. We might even begin to wonder whether it was precisely because they wanted to meet more regularly to develop their 'system' that led the four pre-1717 lodges in London to ask for a Grand Lodge, when in York already it seems that Freemasons there had begun to consider a Grand Lodge of All England. Whether or not it was the fact that Scottish lodges did so meet that led to this development is still a matter for speculation. What is clear is that the development of Freemasonry thus far south of the border had followed a different path to that north of it.

There are three other factors that have yet to be still more fully researched before we can come to any more conclusive judgement. The first reflects the tortured nature of English society throughout the 17th century. It was not just that there were conflicts between Englishmen and Scots. There were bitter feuds between Protestants and Catholics, Anglicans and Presbyterians, Radicals and Conservatives, Royalists and Parliamentarians, landed gentry and men of business. In the midst of all this religious and political controversy there were those who yet longed for a 'place of repose' (Plot's 'meeting on the moors'?), where honest men could meet their counterparts even from opposing camps.

Francis Bacon was but one protagonist of this sort and the fact that he produced the ideal of Solomon's Temple must have suggested the kind of concept that others could build on. Freemasonry in England would hope to create just that kind of neutral meeting ground which the Royal Society later enjoyed. That kind of social mêlée did not exist in contemporary Scotland.

Secondly, even Dr Stevenson mentions that at this period 'men hoped to unlock the mysteries of the distant past. But the search was not simply historical and scientific; in its essence it was a spiritual quest, and so purification and spiritual enlightenment were essential to success . . .' (*The First Freemasons*, p. 6) The effects of the Renaissance were also beginning to be felt in England and the emergence of new groups of landed gentry free to read, travel, and study, alongside even better educated tradesmen and persons in the professions, caused circles of study and enquiry to be formed in which just such 'searches of the past' could be pursued. We even have the evidence of one letter from an émigré German scholar who tells his gentlemen friends that they would do well to sit at the side, or even the feet, of some of their employed craftsmen and acquire their skill and their secrets. The seven liberal arts were being rediscovered. Do we perhaps need to learn much more than we already know about the 'circles' in such houses as those of the Percys, the Herberts, the Cecils or the Sackvilles, to mention but a handful? Have we really exhausted what their family records could tell us? Or what about the diaries of the 'City fathers'? Were there more occasional lodges than we have so far uncovered?

Thirdly, we need to recognise that there may still be an untouched source in late 17th-century England. The present received wisdom is that there are no such records to be uncovered and yet in 1911 the United Grand Lodge of England is on record as stating that undoubtedly part of the working accepted by the Premier Grand Lodge was taken from existing operative practices. Did that mean Scottish operative working, through Dr Anderson, or was it an English source as well, or alone? Recent work of my own suggests that there was some kind of residual operative organisation leading to at least the lodges that appeared in York and Hull in the 18th century. We know of the operative influences between Teesside and the Border and we know something else. There is the fact that whilst it is true that the lodges that met in Warrington and Chester were made up largely of non-operatives, there were operatives in them. This does not mean that English 'lodges' derived from operative ones but it does lend credence to the idea that an operative member or two could assist these gentlemen or traders in the right formation of the gathering which they were creating, for whatever occasional purpose. Even if these were new kinds of Masonic lodge they had to have some obvious connection with past or present lodge practice, otherwise why call them 'lodges' and how could they be recognised as such?

I said at the outset that this would not be a definitive paper. By the very nature of our still limited knowledge it cannot be other than an investigation. What I hope I have done is to clear the ground still further for more useful construction work to be done. What at least seems much more acceptable today is the affirmation that the origins of Scottish and English Freemasonry were different. Exactly how different is the subject for more papers.

THE DEVELOPMENT OF ENGLISH FREEMASONRY FROM 1350 T0 1730

The talk which I am here presenting to you is the direct result of the last few years of research and the writing of one recent week. It is the considered conclusion of a great deal of thinking based on the collection of much new information. Because it at last makes sense of the whole period of Masonic development between 1350 and 1730, it has seemed a worthwhile topic to share with experienced and interested brethren. I shall first lay out the story of this whole period as I have now come to understand it and then close with some remarks on what seem to be its benefits in terms of solving the age-old question: 'Where did our present form of English Freemasonry come from?' I shall then value any comments, criticisms or queries so that I sharpen up what, I hope, will be a useful contribution to Masonic history generally.

I begin with the known form of an operative or building site lodge in the 14th century. It takes its name from a temporary lean-to structure resting against the side of some new erection be it a castle, monastery, church or large house. Its Norman-French name was 'allogement'. In it gathered the workmen known as Fellows or Masters of their crafts — those who squared, shaped, decorated, carved, completed and laid the various pieces of masonry required for the nearby structure. In this 'lodge' they also ate, rested, conversed and gathered for any 'business' and the latter could range from discussing wage-rates to welcoming new colleagues and agreeing who would train the apprentices who were introduced, not by them, but by the Master Masons on the same site. For the fact often overlooked, but now proven by reference to contemporary documents is that this kind of site lodge was ruled, not by a Master Mason, but by a Warden chosen by those Fellows from amongst their number. Indeed, the Master Mason was not even allowed to enter such a lodge though he might recommend apprentices to it and knock on its door when it was time for labour to be resumed. It is very important to discern this separation of the roles between the Master Masons and the Fellows or Master Craftsmen as far as building work was concerned.

Alongside these practical arrangements on a building site we have to note that from at least 1350 there is another form of association for craftsmen masons. This was a Guild/Company which appears in what were then the large cities of England as well as abroad. After 1350, when the ranks of the working craftsmen had been severely depleted by the Black Death, with the result that there was a sharp rise in the wage demands of those that remained, the Crown declared that only recognised Guilds or Trade Companies could regulate wages and so that such Companies might be approved they had to produce evidence of their ancient right to represent their trades, show how old those rights were and thus qualify for a new Royal Charter which gave them the right to operate in their trade.

Thus we note the appearance of such masons' guilds in, e.g. Durham, York, Chester, Coventry, Norwich and London. These Guilds were then ruled over by a Court with a Master and two Wardens, the latter usually called Upper and Lower. Membership of the

Company was only allowed to those craftsmen who qualified as Freemen of the local Borough. The significant difference between this gathering and that on the working site was that in the Guild both Master Masons and Fellows would be able to mingle so long as they were each Freemen locally. In the Guild the Master and Wardens were elected by the members. Each Guild adopted its Trade's Ancient Rules and Regulations, its record of the Craft's history and a Charter. Hence arose the notion that the Freemasons' first Charter was received from King Athelstan around 926 AD. Those admitted to the Guild had long since been apprenticed to their trade and so were at once accepted as Fellows of the Company.

If you ask how we can be so sure about what I have just told you then I have to explain two other things. One is that from 1350 onwards there appear in records still extant some distinctive documents called 'The Old Charges'. The first of these is now known as the Regius MS whilst the second is called the Cooke MS. Both of these were in circulation prior to 1415 and after them came a whole series of similar publications until the middle of the 18th century. Copies of some of these actual documents are in masonic libraries like York.

The other fact is that also from the period of 1375-1400 there took place in the cities I have mentioned public processions of plays put on by these trade Companies. As the Latin word for a 'trade' is 'ministerium', which we English soon called 'misterium', these plays have become known as Mystery Plays. We know that the masons companies put on their plays along with other trades. These plays were produced almost every year for the next 200 years and to give you some idea of what was involved in producing them I should tell you that whilst a Master Mason then received a wage of 40 pence a week each of these plays cost £250 per annum to present.

In the first part of the 1500s the mason trade took some very hard knocks. King Henry VII refused to allow any more castles to be built and even caused many castles to be pulled down or reduced in size. Henry VIII, his son, closed down not only the large and small monasteries and convents but also the hospitals, almshouses and chapels which they maintained. In York some 50 buildings were wholly or partly demolished. Henry's son, Edward VI, closed down the religious guilds, their chapels and special places of prayer, as on bridges, called chantry chapels and all stone altars; whilst in the reign of Elizabeth I even the Mystery Plays were discontinued. It can be imagined how all this legislation affected the working masons. The number of their building sites was greatly diminished and so therefore were the lodges on them. Not only was this the case but we notice in the reign of the Tudors that there was now a preference for building in brick and wood. The idea of a lodge, indeed, was in real danger of dying out.

The masons, however, had another string to their bow. In the cities where they had their trade companies they began to add a lodge to that body. No other trade guild did this, not even the carpenters, who were such close associates of the masons in all medieval building work.

What now happened in at least York and Chester, where we have the evidence from recent research, is interesting. Because there were those in these cities who were deprived of their chapels, their old religious practices, the plays, the saints and parish guilds, they began to look around for other outlets for their piety, their almsgiving and social association.

Compelling evidence of the attraction of this new kind of Freemasonry for those recently deprived of so much religious heritage is provided by the overt reference in the Cooke MS to its source for the Masonic history which it relates. The reader is constantly reminded that what is here recorded is found 'in policronico'. This refers to the 14th century world history, now in nine volumes, which was compiled by the Chester monk, Sir Ranulph Higden, and named 'Polychronicon'. What greater pull could there be for religious traditionalists than to join a Guild or Company which still preserved, as part of its ceremonial working, a text deriving from pre-Reformation Benedictine monasticism.

We know now that by the mid-17th century in York and Chester there were lodges attached to the Mason Trade Guilds into which those who were Freemen of other trades than the building ones were 'accepted' as lodge members. Since they were all Freemen there was no question of there being any need for apprenticeship in such a lodge and so there was initially only one possible grade for the members: that of Fellow. They still met in a lodge ruled over by a Warden. This, incidentally, explains the kind of lodge in which Elias Ashmole was received, 'with Bro. Penketh as Warden' ruling over it.

The important thing to realise is that being a member of such a lodge was not the same as being a member of the Guild. Guild membership was reserved for those in the mason's trade and, of course, any mason in the Company had the right to be a member of the lodge linked to it. Indeed the presence of some working masons in the lodge was essential in order to know how to open and conduct business in a lodge correctly by the old traditions.

What happens now, however, is that slowly but surely the old traditions of the masons are adapted and added to by the traditions that are brought into this new kind of lodge by others. These were they who once had their own religious guild practices, those who had now experienced the new classical education of the grammar schools and the benefit of fresh learning by being able to read the newly published printed books that began to flood this country. Nor is that all. For those being educated in the new Renaissance learning, MSS such as the Cooke included, again from monastic sources, emphasis on for example Hermes, Euclid and Pythagoras. The attraction of ancient knowledge was to persist through persons like Ashmole, Randle Holme and Dr Stukeley.

It is hardly surprising if the working masons began to wonder what the new Guild Lodge Freemasons were starting to do. What also happened is that the style of ruling the Guild Court spread to the lodge so that it too was ruled by a Right Worshipful Master and two Wardens; and the additional knowledge which had been the preserve of the old Master Masons was now able to be shared in this new body. This was made part of the additional knowledge restricted to the Masters of this kind of lodge.

Something else of a practical kind also began to happen. Following the Civil War period of 1645-1660 there was a new desire for two things. One was for a place where the bitterness of political or religious conflict could be avoided and the other was, literally, the rebuilding of a whole society. Only one church was built in England between 1640 and 1660, no substantial homes were built or even maintained, for the gentry were heavily taxed by Parliament, and even battered city walls were left unrepaired. The Restoration of the monarchy, the return of noble families to their homes and the emergence of more merchants because of more profitable trade meant that there was a resurgence of the need for stonemasons. The Great Fire of London, 1666, was not only a major spur to rebuilding in the capital but also elsewhere. The masons' trade started afresh even though the bricklayers and carpenters were also in much demand. This leads us on to the next stage of our story.

As the demand for new building and repair grew so did the renewed expectations of the working mason trade. The return to the previous standards of professional workmanship and the need to regulate wages and terms of employment meant that there was a revived need for a recognised trade body to which the operative masons could belong and which would serve their day to day needs. What became clear is that though in York and Chester there already existed such a company from late medieval times it was not now regarded as adequate or appropriate for the needs of contemporary stonemasons. That is why, in both cities in the latter 17th century, there was an application to the municipal authority for another charter to found a Mason Company. Sadly we do not know from the extant documentation why these operatives chose to disregard the older body bearing their name but it would seem as if the activities of their attached 'lodges' had begun to outweigh and even overshadow the original purpose of the Company to which they were attached. In any event the municipal authorities of York and Chester saw fit to accede to the application made to them and charters were granted, though in both cities the masons were required to include in their new companies allied trades such as bricklayers, carpenters or blacksmiths. As far as the actual tradesmen were concerned their previous links with the old Guild were now severed.

What this meant for the 'speculative' Freemen members of the old Mason's Company lodge was that to all intents and purposes the 'Lodge' was now to become an independent body which no longer looked to a parent Guild for oversight or reference. The era of the independent private 'Masonic Lodge' was about to dawn. It would inevitably lead to three clear changes.

It meant first of all that the new kind of lodge had to discover a fresh type of governance. It was now removed from the connection with municipal oversight that necessarily went with a Guild attachment. In York this had a singular result. We know that from the registers of 1705 at least the lodge regarded itself as a self-governing body which was acting as a form of Grand Lodge in the older operative sense. This meant that it believed it had the power to recreate itself in other parts of its old operative territory, north of the River Trent and to authorise gentlemen in Scarborough or Bradford to meet as 'Freemasons' following the customs, and considering themselves as an extension, of the York parent body.

In Chester the development was different. As the older Guild Lodge members died off by 1700 some of their relatives and colleagues appear to have decided to continue a private lodge which by 1725 was, says brand new evidence, so large that it was divided into three such bodies, all with differing types of membership. For their authority they turned to the newly developing Grand Lodge of 1717 in London and Westminster and were entered on the latter's register. I am currently studying what pattern of change was followed by the 17th century lodges in Chichester, West Sussex, or Coventry.

The second change concerned the nature of membership. As you may recall the Guild Lodges required potential members to be Freemen of their locality. When the lodges discontinued their association with a Guild or Company this requirement no longer pertained. Hence the door to membership was open to anyone who was considered 'a fit and proper person' by the members of a respective lodge. If, however, it was no longer the case that a candidate had to be a Freeman of some trade the question arose as to whether he had ever been an apprentice as tradition required. The need for some kind of ceremonial Apprenticeship therefore now became evident and it is thus hardly surprising that such a grade of membership was newly introduced after 1717 though it is noticeable that even in London the Grand Lodge clearly regarded this as such a novelty that it left such an introductory step for each lodge to perform privately. What it did encourage, as was not the case in York, was a separate opening of a lodge in the grade of Apprentice where that was to be conferred. Under the Grand Lodge of All England at York, throughout the 18th century, its lodges only normally opened in one degree, that of Fellow.

The third change was in regard to the ceremony of admission. Whereas York, as in the Guild Lodges, used the Old Charges, Regulation and History as the main content of this act of entry and thus recognised a new Freemason as being a 'Mason of the Craft', the growing tendency in the South was to begin to regard a candidate as a member of the Premier Grand Lodge, accepting the Constitutions devised by Dr Anderson. What is to be noted is that when a further Grand Lodge began in 1751 its founders claimed that they were seeking to follow the Ancient Constitutions according to the Charter of King Athelstan at York in 926. This is precisely why they were called 'Antients'. What was also a constant 18th century practice in York was that admission to the Craft did not automatically mean admission to membership of a lodge. A separate vote had to be taken to make the latter possible. The old distinction between being a member of the Mason Trade and being a member of a Mason's lodge was still retained. That idea soon faded under the London dispensation.

What I have sought to provide for us is a clearer picture of how English Freemasonry developed from an operative practice to the form of Freemasonry to which we have become accustomed. This narrative, based on all the available evidence, suggests not only that our development was a natural one but that it was different from that which took place north of the Border. I would also point out that the two developments are not successive but contemporary and at a time when little love was lost between the two neighbouring nations. What has not been available hitherto is any easy access to the story of the emergence of a Freemasonry in England that was more than a single initiation of Elias Ashmole in 1646. The fact is that there is much more to our Masonic history than that. When we know that, as I have, I hope, begun to intimate, we are able to appreciate much more about where we came from and hence who we really are. When a W. Master invites a Warden to check the door of his lodge, or when the W. Master invites a Warden to close the lodge, we are reverting to a period way back beyond 1717. We are also back in those earlier days when an Installing Master opens in the Fellow's degree because it was only there that a ruler was elected and obligated in medieval days. (Note that changing the term Fellow to Fellowcraft was a later Scottish import.) When, however, the Master Elect is asked for an assent to the Ancient Charges and Regulations we are back in a Guild Lodge with a Master Mason about to be in charge. Such, my brethren, are just a few glimpses of what knowing about our true past can provide. Of course it is also perfectly right and sensible to live in the present but only if we really know who and where we are?

THE GRAND LODGE OF ALL ENGLAND AT YORK AND THE YORK RITE — A FRESH APPRAISAL

Were you to question any average English or Welsh Freemason today about the topic of this paper, you would, I strongly suspect, be greeted with complete and utter astonishment. This would not be because such a brother could not conceive of there being anything new to be said about the subject but because he would not know anything about the subject at all. If he had done any Masonic reading, or been to a certain number of lectures, or even listened carefully when a United Grand Lodge certificate is presented, he might have grasped that in the 18th century there were two Grand Lodges that were at work in England and Wales, the one started in 1717 and called the Premier (or later, Moderns) Grand Lodge, and another, begun in 1751, which called itself the Antients Grand Lodge. That would be the extent of his awareness of such matters.

That there was ever a Grand Lodge of All England at York, let alone a Grand Lodge South of the River Trent, both in the 18th century, and that there is still a *York Rite*, would astonish and confuse him. It might even be having just that effect on some who are present today. Before I therefore start on some of the fresh things that can now be said about this topic, it is as well that I introduce you to some of the things that have so far been written. When we understand just how this York Freemasonry was previously regarded we will the more usefully appreciate such new insights as are now possible.

Anyone who has studied the emergence of the Antients Grand Lodge will know its founders had one principal objective. They sought to restore in England, and especially in the south of the country, a form of Freemasonry that they believed was more in tune with the traditional teachings and practices of the Craft. What those teachings and practices were and what the Antients did to achieve their aims has been well, and often, told elsewhere and is not our concern here. What is important to record is that in the book of Constitutions acknowledged by the Antients, *Ahiman Rezon*, Laurence Dermott says that the 'Antient' masons were called 'York Masons' because of the claim that Prince Edwin obtained a Royal Charter which permitted the first Grand Lodge to congregate in the city of York in 926 AD.

Of this claim Bernard Jones has written as follows (p. 215):

'Dermott was repeating a *myth* ... Well aware of the *halo surrounding York masonry*, he flagrantly borrowed an appellation which he *shrewdly believed* would render indelible *the stamp of antiquity* which he had skilfully affixed to the "Antients" system — a stamp *whose genuineness we see no reason to question seriously*, but which has not gained *added authenticity* by association with the white rose of York.'

Whilst we shall consider this argument carefully in a moment, we must note that this is not the whole of the evidence. There is also the opinion of Lionel Vibert, who wrote this:

'Yorkshire, perhaps more than any other locality outside London, preserved in *scattered communities*, remaining in touch with one another, the *old traditions and usages* of the Craft, until the time came when they were to be handed on to those who *developed from them* our freemasonry as it is today.'

He concluded:

'If the phrase *"York Masonry"* be understood to imply, not that the users of it belonged only to York, but merely that *in common with the Brethren of that city* they adhered to the *ancient customs of the Order* and valued its old traditions, no harm will be taken. We can still talk of "York Masonry" in that sense; we can recognise that York, in the Craft, still implies a high standard, a reverence for our time-immemorial customs, and the preservation of all that is best in freemasonry today.'

These statements require to be examined more carefully to see exactly what they are saying. They certainly raise the following questions which we must address:

1. Why was there a *'halo surrounding York Masonry'*, especially if the Edwin story was a *myth*?
2. If claiming an attachment to York would *not* add to the undoubted genuineness of Dermott's claim to the Antients' antiquity, then why is he called *shrewd* in doing so?
3. What were these *'scattered communities'* that kept in touch with one another, and in which *'old traditions and usages'* were preserved?
4. Who were the people who *'developed'* those traditions, and into which present Freemasonry did they develop it?

I believe that as you allow me to respond to these important queries we shall both get into the heart of our subject and also look at it with fresh eyes and fresh material.

The source of the York 'halo'
I begin to deal with this issue by referring to something that is still often overlooked by my contemporaries. It is the fact that already in the period of at least 1725 to 1740 there was a groundswell of dissatisfaction with the development of the newer forms of Craft Masonry. This happened a substantial time *before* the Antients Grand Lodge came on the scene and the groundswell revealed itself in at least two distinct areas, one around the City of London and one in the north-east of England.

The catechisms that developed in the south are today enshrined in the ceremonies of the *Royal Order of Scotland*, whilst the lectures that developed from catechisms in the north-east formed the *Harodim* tradition which, as we shall see, formed a basis for all the subsequent degrees comprising the York Rite. We have therefore *in situ* by 1743, a whole decade before the emergence of the Antients Grand Lodge, a Masonic tradition of working that claimed antique origins, proper preservation of biblical and legendary traditions, and a span of instruction that admitted Apprentices and could also make them qualified Masters of the Craft, including an *Arch* element.

As the later name of this process in the south implies, the English roots of the Royal

keystone, is set on top of them. The Master takes the keystone, steps up on a chair and sets it in its proper place, and drives it down with six raps of the gavel.

There, at last, is the ceremony of the Arch degree that we have been seeking.

That is also why, in most Royal Arch chapters that meet away from London, you will find some kind of Arch with real keystones or archstones at the head and, across the arch, words such as: *Fiat Lux et Lux Fuit* ('Let there be Light and there was Light').

In January 1810 we discover an interesting minute in the Minerva Chapter of Kingston-upon-Hull. It reads: 'A material change and alteration took place in the Chapter this evening, namely the introduction of the Arch with "Holiness to the Lord" painted in gold letters thereon, in front of the three M.E. Grands. The Pedestal and Master's Level, with appropriate inscriptions in Brass letters thereon, and the Burning Bush within and under the said Arch, *being the first introduction of these essential requisites* in this part of the United Kingdom . . .'

In his comment on this innovation, Bernard Jones wrote: 'Is it possible that some ideas were being borrowed from a travelling *military* lodge or were introduced by an *Irish* visitor?' (p. 161). In view of what has already been stated above, it does indeed seem a likely suggestion.

For those Royal Arch Masons who have such an item this is an ample reminder of a part of Freemasonry that was once a distinctive and essential element in the Royal Arch ceremonies but which in England and Scotland is now absorbed by talk of *a crypt or vault*.

With all this evidence before us it might be worth considering afresh the earliest form of *Arch* ceremony to which Dr Oliver refers in his book, *Origin of the Royal Arch* (pp. 86ff). In the first section of the Rite he describes, the three candidates approach the Right Worshipful Master's chair: 'Sire, the Temple being now finished and dedicated . . . we are anxious to obtain that distinguished reward . . . of being admitted into the honourable degree of Geometrick Master Masons.'

On the return of Hiram, King of Tyre, this is done and search is made for the absent Hiram Abif. Oliver continues: 'After certain ceremonies (describing journeys) the Brethren made their report. *Then followed a representation of the Arch, and the recovery of the Lost Word.*' Oliver concludes: 'Such was the outline of the Royal Arch, as a completion of the Third Degree . . . although the plan was subsequently extended by *the addition* of the cavern and its mysterious contents . . .'

There are, before we close, three other pieces of evidence that need to be considered by anyone who might still have doubts about the thesis which I have introduced. The first is that so-called Operative *Lodges* in Scotland invariably use an Arch as the motif for their banners. The second is that in Scottish chapters to this day a pillared Arch is set up as the focus of their ceremony and an Arch degree ceremony is still listed as being under the auspices of the Supreme Grand Chapter of that land. And thirdly, in the Province of Northumberland, in the 1820s, we have Certificates appointing brethren to Provincial Office showing what look amazingly like the very Arch, Ark of the Covenant and Altar of incense features that suggest an Arch and Royal Arch connection.

What we have here uncovered begins to answer some of those persistent questions which so often puzzle Companions. How is the Royal Arch the completion of the Master's degree? Where does this Arch with its keystone come from? Why do we have an Arch rather than a dome? Why do Irish Royal Arch Masons still persist in keeping to an Arch and another legend, whilst we follow a different path? Where did the Ark of the Covenant and the ceremony of the Veils fit in? All these things at last begin to be much clearer once you have recognised the Arch Degree.

If you then want to know where the domed vault, the rebuilding of the temple, and the pedestal secrets came from you are simply asking for yet another lecture.

THE GENEVA BIBLE AND ITS CONTRIBUTION TO THE DEVELOPMENT OF ENGLISH RITUAL

Some time ago, I was invited to give this paper at the oldest lodge still meeting in Geneva, Switzerland. It was a subject that had lingered in my mind for a considerable time and I was delighted to be provided at last with the opportunity to give the first presentation to an appreciative audience in the very city associated with this particular form of the Volume of the Sacred Law. No other paper had ever been presented on the topic, although the late Harry Carr did make three brief references to the Geneva Bible in his compendious *Freemason at Work* and another Past Master of Quatuor Coronati Lodge, Christopher Haffner, gave it an honourable mention in his book, *Workman Unashamed*, so the matter has not been wholly overlooked.

It might be claimed that since this subject has not attracted substantial attention thus far it is probably not one that deserves even the scope of one whole lecture. That is something you will have to judge for yourselves when I have finished. I can only state that whereas I started out with the certainty that there would be at least enough to occupy us for this one evening, I now know that there is other material which I cannot share with you today and a much longer and, I believe, equally interesting paper could with ease be presented if time were available. Let me however start to whet your appetite by what is available and in order that we all begin from the same point I must describe briefly the historical background of this work.

It was in the reign of Henry VIII that the first copies of a whole Bible made their appearance in the parish churches of England. This was called the *Great* Bible, otherwise and in some later editions called the *Bishops'* Bible, and it was in 1540 that chained copies — chained because they were too precious and costly to allow them to be purloined by an eager new readership — were authorised to be set on lecterns for open reading to the congregation. That version of the Bible was largely dependent on the work done by another English refugee on the Continent, William Tyndale. (I note with some pride that he was a member of the same Oxford College as I was later to attend.) This Bible continued to have use and pride of place throughout the short but even more reformed reign of Edward VI.

From 1553 to 1558 Mary was on the throne and one of her early decisions was that such Bibles must be removed from churches as the services were once more to be recited in Latin. Whilst some died for their reformed beliefs during her reign, others sought refuge once more overseas, initially in the Netherlands but also in German cities, such as Frankfurt. It was from Frankfurt, in 1555, that a particular band of Englishmen and their families made their way to Geneva, where a determined effort was being made to create a city governed by Reformed Christian principles. Indeed so precise was the concern of its rulers — the *seniores* or elders — that no one was admitted by this date unless satisfactorily vouched for. The English refugees had to undergo the same test as all others.

To be exact the contingent that came in November of 1555 had been preceded by 20 persons belonging to the family of Sir William Stafford, an English nobleman who was of such close royal descent that it was deemed advisable for him to be abroad whilst Mary was on the throne.

Yet it was the 27 people who were headed by William Whittingham and the formidable John Knox who require our notice. On 14 November 1555 the Council of Geneva granted these ministers and their families the church of *Ste Marie-le-Noue* for their sole use on Mondays, Tuesdays and Wednesdays, whilst on Sundays they shared it with the Waldensian Christians who came from what today we would call Northern Italy. These latter had the church for their sole use during the rest of the week.

From a remarkable record called *Le Livre des Anglois* (The English Folks' book), which is now kept in the Town Hall at Geneva, we can discover who made up this first wave of temporary residents. We note, in addition to the two already mentioned, William Williams and Thomas Wood, Christopher Goodman and Anthony Gilby. This last-named person was in due course to be very closely associated with the City of Leicester, and all of them were to be the principal translators of the Geneva Bible from the Hebrew and Greek.

Their leader, William Whittingham, was born in Chester in 1524 and educated in Oxford. He settled down so well in Geneva that he married a sister of John Calvin himself. The following testimony that he left tells us how he and the other English folk were received in their exile.

'But to the end that we might be delivered from insupportable tyranny God hath provided better for us insomuch that He hath moved the Magistrates' hearts towards us in granting us a church at Geneva — where God's word is truly preached, manners best reformed, and in earth the chiefest place of true comfort.'

Allen Hinds, in his book *The Making of Elizabethan England*, adds to our understanding of the background:

'This Genevan church was formed of men of a very great strength of character [so that] of all the churches founded abroad by the English at this time, this alone produced works of permanent importance.'

There was gathered here, says another writer (James Packer, then Principal of Tynedale Hall, Bristol) 'a galaxy of Reformation men who were themselves true Renaissance individualists, rugged, heroic, cantankerous, whimsical and tender by turns, with fighting and exploring instincts well developed, ready both to travel and to suffer, if need be, for the cause of God and truth.'

He continues (vol 3, pp. 7, 8):

'On the title page of the 1560 Geneva Bible is a woodcut which shows the Israelites standing with their backs to the Red Sea gazing in terror at the advancing Egyptians [who seem to be] only a few yards away. BUT, behind them, over the sea, rises the pillar of cloud (The Israelites will see it the moment they turn their backs) and along the edges of the picture run the texts: "Feare ye not, stand stil, and behold the salvacion of the Lord . . ." "The Lord shall fight for you . . ." "Great are the troubles of the righteous: but the Lord deliuereth them out of all" . . . [These Geneva men] were what they were because

for these two 16th-century 'balls' (*gooloth* in the original Hebrew) to be steadily transformed into the spheres which now adorn our pillars on Wardens' pedestals or on the 2° tracing boards. Yet it was the first pictures in the Geneva Bible which started the idea.

Again, it is only in the Geneva Bible that we at last realise where the side 'chambers' come from in which the workmen went to be paid their wages. In the accompanying illustration they were in three storeys alongside the inner temple buildings and to get to these chambers you had to mount stairs inside the temple and not from any outside door.

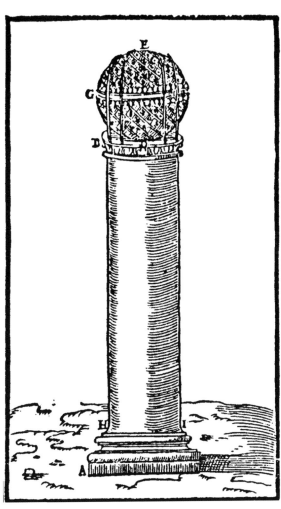

THE FORME OF THE
PILLER.

A B The ueight of a pillert eighten cubit:s:the compaffe of a piller was twelue cubites.
D E The height of the chapiter or rounde balle vpö the piller of fiue cubits height.
G In ȳ middes were two rowes of pomegranates: ȳ reft is the networke & flowred lices or roses.

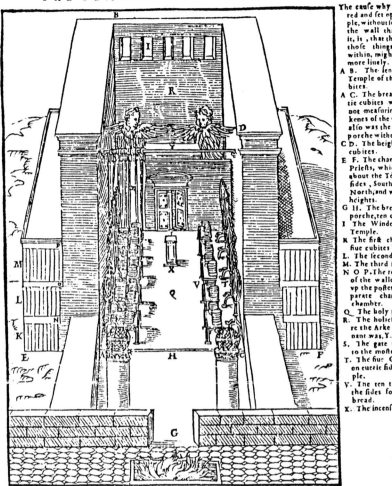

The caufe why we recoue-
red and fet open the Te-
ple, without fettig forth
the wall that is before
it, is, that the ordre of
thofe things that are
within, might be fene
more liuely.

A B. The length of the
Temple of threefcore cu-
bites.

A C. The breadth of twe-
tie cubites within, and
not meafuring the thic-
kenes of the walles. This
alfo was the length of f
porche without f Teple.

C D. The height of thirtie
cubites.

E F. The chambers of the
Priefts, which copaffed
about the Teple on thre
fides, South, Weft and
North; and were of thre
heights.

G H. The breadth of the
porche, ten cubites.

I The Windowes of the
Temple.

K The firft chamber was
fiue cubites broad.

L. The feconde fix.

M. The third feuen.

N O P. The refts or ftayes
of the walle, which bare
vp the poftes that did fe-
parate chamber from
chamber.

Q The holy place

R. The holieft of all, where the Arke of the coue-
nant was, Y.

S. The gate to enter in-
to the mofte holy place.

T. The fiue Candelftickes
on euerie fide of the Te-
ple.

V. The ten tables on bo-
the fides for the fhewe
bread.

X. The incenfe altar.

In the same fashion we also grasp from the drawing of the Holy of Holies why there was apparent confusion over the windows, or dormers, 'that gave light to the same'. The text suggests that the Sanctum Sanctorum was totally dark, but here we have it enlightened by five windows high up in the wall. That must have really tested interpreters.

The picture of the Throne of Solomon is also intriguing. We see a figure approaching the monarch who is above seven steps and between two more pillars. The throne is under a rounded canopy which is adorned with three inverted squares. At the foot of the steps is a 'chequered pavement' which continued the normal medieval form of pavement shown in earlier manuscripts. The dome-shaped niche and canopied seat is almost identical with Master's places still in Weymouth and Taunton.

The feature of the 'Arch of Heaven' is a principal item in the last of these woodcuts at the start of the Book of Ezekiel. This picture reveals a figure in a familiar Royal Arch attitude under a cloudy canopy with four wheels that resemble astrolabes, four beasts with different faces, and God sitting upon a throne but also on the arch of a rainbow.

Such, all too briefly, are a few of the visual effects that this very remarkable English Bible introduced into the cultural life of the 17th-century folk that were, in part, to establish English speculative Freemasonry. Of course, it is true that once the general impact of the Geneva Bible editions had been assimilated and underlined, as well as enhanced, by the sonorous language and fine scholarship of the next great translation, it was possible to lose sight of the contribution that had been made by those refugee scholars. The sheer weight of Royal Authority given to the King James 1611 version and the events that followed the Restoration of 1662 were such that for a while its predecessor went into retirement — a state of affairs that now needs to be carefully reviewed. Whilst not wanting to claim overmuch for this source-book of ideas and symbols, I would, I think, be not unjustified in saying that without the Geneva Bible our Masonic heritage would have been different and might well have been much less memorable. For the moment I rest my case.

WHAT WAS DUNCKERLEY
PLAYING AT?

On 1 September 1769 in the George Tavern at Portsmouth something rather unusual took place. At a meeting of the Royal Arch Chapter held under the auspices of the Phoenix Lodge the Provincial Grand Master, Thomas Dunckerley, Esq. 'brought the Warrant of the Chapter and having lately received "the Mark" he made the brethren Mark Masons and Mark Masters and each chose their "Mark"'. He also told the members about the cipher style of writing to be used in the Mark degrees, which could be shared with Fellowcrafts if they were to be Mark Masons and with Master Masons if they wished to become Mark Masters.

This was a remarkable occurrence and not only because it is still the only substantial record of the introduction of the Mark degrees into English 18th century Freemasonry. What is even more remarkable is the setting in which these events took place and the person who was instrumental in bringing them about. Who was this gentleman, Thomas Dunckerley, and why was it especially surprising that it should be he who introduced such new Masonic activity?

Thomas was born on 23 October 1724 in a house attached to one of the royal residences either in London or Richmond, Surrey. He was delivered by the midwife to the Royal Family because, as Thomas only discovered 36 years later, he was the illegitimate son of George II. This fact being discreetly concealed during his youth the boy had apparently to seek his own future and accordingly he sought a career in the Navy. By 1760 he appears as the Master Gunner on HMS *Vanguard* as she sailed down the St. Lawrence River to assist the assault on Quebec that has ever since been associated with the name of General Wolfe. By 1764 he was superannuated and his Naval service was over and though he was now aware of his origins and had a 'pride that rose superior to what my station had been in the Navy' he was also heavily in debt and desperate to know how he would manage. Eventually in 1767 he began to receive a pension from the Crown and was then granted a Grace and Favour apartment at Hampton Court. Despite all his anxieties his loyalty to the Crown never seems to have wavered and his status as at least a part-Royal now served him in good stead as a Mason.

He was ever a devoted and trusted member of the Premier Grand Lodge. Proof of this is revealed in the circumstances surrounding his engagement in North America. When he appears on HMS *Vanguard* he is also in possession of a document from the Moderns Grand Lodge. This was a warrant of 1760, No. 254, which authorized him 'to hold a Lodge and make Masons on board' his ship. But this was not all. He also had authority to create the first English Provincial Grand Lodge on that continent and on 24 June 1760 installed the Hon. Simon Fraser, Colonel of the 78th Highland Regiment, as Provincial Grand Master of Canada. Dunckerley was therefore known and highly regarded in his Grand Lodge back home and was adding to his reputation by becoming the first ambassador for English Freemasonry across the Atlantic and also a noted pioneer of Freemasonry at sea.

What we also need to know is that Dunckerley had been initiated at Portsmouth in 1754 and one of the people who drew him into the Craft was the same Lord Chesterfield whose 'Letters to his Son' have ever since been one of the leading pieces of 18th century literature. When he returned to his Plymouth home he joined Masonry there, becoming not only a member of two lodges but Right Worshipful Master of both in 1756. Not only was he an assiduous traveller in order to attend at both places but he was a careful student of the catechismal lectures which then formed the core of what we now call the degree ceremonies. He even wrote a pamphlet, 'The Light and Truth of Masonry Explained' in which he began to express his convictions about what the Craft was and the direction it should be taking.

It can thus be seen that in Thomas Dunckerley the Grand Lodge of the Moderns had both a staunch supporter but also a dedicated promoter. He was increasingly seen as an experienced brother and a person of some status and influence who could be relied on to enhance the position and future of Freemasonry according to the Moderns landmarks and Constitutions. Or could he? Was his attitude fully in accord with that of the Grand Lodge to which he owned allegiance?

In order to answer that question we need to know a little more about the state of English Freemasonry by the middle years of the 18th century. In particular we need to appreciate what was the difference between the two Grand Lodge bodies that are referred to so often, the Antients and the Moderns.

Two simple indications that they were different are seen in two things that we do nowadays. The first is the way in which the Worshipful Master and Wardens sit in the lodge room and the way they sit at the Festive Board. The former position is the way they originally sat in an Antients lodge room whilst the latter is the way they sat in a Moderns lodge room. If you go to the Netherlands and attend a lodge there you will see that as they received their Freemasonry from the Moderns that is why they still have the two wardens sitting in the West alongside the two great pillars, B. and J.

The other feature that reveals their difference is marked by the use of two words in the exchange of secrets in the Third Degree. We have two because one was that used by the Antients and the other was that used by the Moderns. Again, if you attend a Third Degree ceremony in the Netherlands you will find that they only use one word, that which they took from Moderns' practice. If you don't know which that was you can write to me care of the publishers to enquire.

That there were distinct differences between the practices of the two Grand Lodges is therefore beyond question. Yet it was not only the small matters that differed. What was much more important was the clear difference regarding the content of what we would call degrees. Let me explain.

The Antients who were formed as a Grand Lodge in 1751 were aware that there had been an older tradition of Masonry in the 17th century which differed noticeably from that which was devised and presented by the Premier Grand Lodge of 1717. This older form of Freemasonry was based on a form of Lodge which was attached to a Guild or Trade Company of Stonemasons and entrance to which required its members to be Freemen of the City in which the Guild existed. Because they were already Freemen they must have already been apprentices and so this form of Lodge only met in one degree, that of Fellow. May I here remind you that the term Fellowcraft is a Scottish term and only came into English Masonry after 1717.

When, however, the old Guilds ceased to function and the lodges attached to them in e.g. York, Chester, Coventry and London, were left to operate on their own the requirement of being a 'Freeman' of a Trade generally ceased and so there was the need to restore an apprentice grade. What may interest you to know is that in the Grand Lodge of All England at York that had Minute Books going back at least to the end of the 17th century there was never a separate lodge opening for Apprentices but they were made Apprentices and Fellows on the same evening in a lodge opened in the Fellow grade. That is why when even the Premier Grand Lodge began it recognised only that degree though it very soon approved an Opening in private lodges for the separate admittance of Apprentices.

There was, however, something else. The main bulk of what we would call the ceremonies consisted of dialogue-exchanges between the Worshipful Master or a Past Master and the members of the lodge seated around a table in the centre of the room. These 'lectures' as they were called, were based on the old history of Freemasonry contained in the Old Charges that were also used for the obligation of a candidate for the Craft. These exchanges began to be quite lengthy by the start of the 18th century and they included references to what we today would think of as Mark, Royal Ark Mariner, Royal Arch, Cryptic and some of the Allied degrees. All this information was regarded as part and parcel of the Craft, though some of it was reserved for those who had passed the Worshipful Master's chair. In due course these lectures became so lengthy that they were split up into different parts and so began the practice of separate degrees. For the Antients all this material was part of being a Masonic lodge. For the Moderns it was not. They believed that the only material to be used was that for the basic degrees of Apprentice and Fellow with the Master Mason degree being added 20 years later. That is why, when a Grand Secretary of the Moderns was approached for charity by an Irish Mason in the 1760s he refused him because, he said: 'We are not Arch, Royal Arch or Antient'. If you want help, he inferred, go to the other body because that is where you belong.

The point that I hope I am now making clear to you is that what principally distinguished the Antients from the Moderns was that the Antients practised a much more complete range of Freemasonry than the Moderns and that is again reflected in the Netherlands where, to this day, they recognise only the first three degrees and nothing else. That was the Moderns' stance and warranted members and lodges of that Grand Lodge were naturally expected to follow their line.

Now, perhaps, you can see where the puzzle of Thomas Dunckerley's behaviour begins to appear. He was a member, a recognised and trusted leader in the Moderns Grand Lodge and yet here he was bringing the charter of a Royal Arch Chapter to Portsmouth and in addition introducing the Mark Mason and Mark Master degrees that he had picked up somewhere else. How and why would he do this? He had taken his obligations in a lodge accepting the rule of the Premier Grand Lodge and was therefore bound by their Constitutions and Regulations. What was he playing at? It is a question that has often been asked.

The answer lies in his strong Service connections. Even on board ship he not only met fellow sailors but he also came into contact with the Marines. We know that from as early as the 1730s military lodges were granted travelling warrants so that they could meet wherever was convenient according to their military service. What is more these warrants were, at this date, all granted by either the Irish Grand Lodge or that of the Antients. When these lodges met they therefore practised any degree that existed under their lodge warrant. When Dunckerley visited these military lodges, and in Active Service conditions no one bothered to ask more than 'Are you a Mason?' before admission, he began to see the attraction of so much that had by now been excluded from the Moderns form of the Craft. Increasingly, and especially as he was made aware of the Old Traditions of the York Masons, which is what the Antients now called themselves, he was convinced that if the Premier Grand Lodge did not associate itself with some of these other aspects of Freemasonry it would lose ground to what was clearly the pulling power of the Antients. He might of course have taken the step of forsaking the Moderns and of becoming an Antients member but if you recall his royal background and the trust he had acquired from the Moderns it is not surprising that he decided on another course. It has also to be recalled that he was a man of 'pride' and we know that he had great ambitions. The only course he could follow was that of persuading his colleagues in the Moderns Grand Lodge that for their own good and because it was likely to prove a fruitful way forward for their membership they should begin to permit some of the neglected aspects of the Old Tradition to be practised in their lodges whilst fashioning them in ways that would be satisfactory to their own requirements.

The astonishing thing is that he was so successful. We have heard what a Moderns Grand Secretary was saying in the 1760s but by the 1770s there was a Supreme Grand Chapter of which that official was the Grand Scribe. Dunckerley had now rewritten the Mark degrees that he had first introduced into a Moderns chapter so that what we have in the Mark degrees today owes a good deal to what he proposed.

Further than that he was the main promoter of the Knightly degrees in England so that what again we know as the Knight Templar, the Knights of Malta and the Red Cross of Constantine have all benefited from his early outlines. Moreover, it was Thomas Dunckerley who sought to revive the ancient Noachic elements of English Freemasonry in Ark Masonry so as to have a naval counterpart to the military Knights orders. That never took off but it did give ideas for those who later revived the degree of Ark Mariner. It can be seen that in an amazing way Thomas Dunckerley changed the face of later 18th century Freemasonry so that even when the Union came it took account of those elements other than the three basic degrees and provided for their continuance when the time was ripe.

What has not been mentioned so far is the sheer physical effect that Dunckerley exercised in order to achieve his goal. Not surprisingly he was made Provincial Grand Master of Hampshire in 1767 but he was subsequently also appointed to Essex Isle of Wight, Dorset, Wiltshire, Somerset, Bristol and Gloucestershire, with Herefordshire as the last. Not only did he hold these appointments but he was Grand Superintendent in no less than 18 Provinces. He was therefore not just a mouthpiece but an activator. His personal interest in, and close attention to, the development of multi-degree Freemasonry led largely to what we see and know today. What it all meant was that when the time for the Union of the Grand Lodges came there was a much wider spectrum to deal with than there would have been had he not exerted the influence which he did.

Mention was made earlier of the pamphlet which Dunckerley wrote as he began to make an impression on the Freemasonry of his day. If we really want to know what he was up to we can hardly do better than allow him to speak to us in his own words:

'What a secret satisfaction it is to Masons, when in searching for Truth, they find the rudiments of all useful knowledge still preserved amongst us, as it has descended by oral tradition from the earliest age; and to find likewise this Truth corroborated by the testimonies of the best and greatest men the world has produced. But this is not all: the Sacred Writings confirm what I assert, the sublime part of our Antient Mystery being there to be found . . . Continue, My Brethren, to preserve in principles that are disinterested, and I doubt not but you will find these rooms which we have now opened and dedicated to Masonry constantly resorted to by the wise, the faithful and the good.' (Chudley, pp. 140-1)

So spoke one who, as his successor as Provincial Grand Master of Essex declared, 'may be considered to have been (a true) father of the Craft'.

FURTHER REFLECTIONS ON THE THIRD DEGREE PUZZLE

Having attempted in a chapter of my recent book *I Just Didn't Know That* to highlight the apparent inconsistencies and queries raised by the ritual of the Third Degree it may come as something of a surprise for you to hear me say that since that piece was written I have realised that what I then said was far from the whole of the story. Research in Freemasonry, as I should by now realise, is an ongoing process and in this particular case nothing could be more true. Whilst what I wrote earlier is still as valid as I then thought what has emerged in my thinking and searching since has made me all the more certain that what we have in our Master Mason degree is even more puzzling than I suggested. It is puzzling, at least, unless we are prepared to recognise that this is not a wholly satisfying step in Masonry but merely part of an unfinished whole. When I read, as I did in a recent Grand Lodge Quarterly Communication, that the Third Degree is complete in itself I just have to say, 'I beg to differ'. What follows reveals more of my reason for taking such a stand.

Ever since my first essay in this field appeared I have wrestled with the question, 'Why in the opening of this degree does the W.M. raise the matter of proceeding from the East to the West?'. Whatever does he mean by saying that? And what is the import of these words, particularly when attached to the reply of a Warden: 'To seek for that which is lost which, by YOUR [presumably the W.M.'s] instruction and our own industry [some rituals say 'endeavours'] we hope to find'? Where is the place of, and what are, the lost secrets which an Installed Master is specially able to reveal to us? Nor is that all for when the W.M. responds later saying, 'We will assist you to REPAIR that loss, and may heaven aid our UNITED endeavours' it surely looks as if the W.M. alone cannot restore the loss that he promises to remedy but needs the help of others. Who are the 'they' that need to unite in order to FULFIL the hope of the brethren? If you tell me that it is the Wardens who assist the W.M. to raise the candidate then why do they not then discover the lost secret? It must be others to whom the W.M. is referring.

Bearing in mind my particular religious affiliation I have been aware for 40 years that at almost the same period as the supposed emergence of the Third Degree (after 1726) there was being practised in London a form of Freemasonry, the Royal Order, which stated, and indeed still states, that the ultimate word and goal of the Craft was made known in what was found in a stable at Bethlehem. It is perhaps natural to assume that thinking of the Three Wise Men who came from the East to the West to visit the family there, this was the likely source of the Third Degree opening idea. But when you think more about that as a possible solution problems arise. The opening ritual, as we have it, was formulated after the 1813 Union of Grand Lodges and a specifically Christian interpretation would have been avoided and certainly not intended. In any case what could be the relevance of such an interpretation where we are thinking of Hiram Abi still seeking to complete the work of building the Temple of Solomon? There has to be another explanation and at the end of last year I at last uncovered what I am sure is the answer.

It was whilst I was in the midst of reading a very new theological book called 'The Great High Priest'. This book seeks to show that the central act of Christian worship, the Holy Communion or Eucharist, is based on the Jewish rituals of the Feast of the Atonement, called by them Yom Kippur, which has as its focus the Holy of Holies in the Temple. It was when the author spoke of this Sanctum Sanctorum as the repository of all God's secrets that the solution of our Masonic Third Degree problem presented itself.

The reason why this solution can be so easily overlooked is because of the way we orientate our present Masonic rooms. We enter them at the West and move towards the W.M.'s place in the East. The Jewish Temple, however, was orientated in exactly the opposite manner. Hence, to discover the true and ultimate secrets of the complete M.M. degree we have to pass from the East by the porchway or entrance of the Holy Place, between the pillars of Boaz and Jachin, to the foot of Jacob's ladder, up the winding staircase to the middle chamber and thence via The Holy Place to the entrance of the Holy of Holies. Here, in the West, we penetrate the blue, purple, crimson and white veil of that entrance and so enter the repository of the Divine Name. Here the angels or Cherubim spread their wings, in a triangular shape, over the Ark of the Covenant on whose golden surface or plate God was said to descend as the Shekinah. That is the journey which the W.M., representing King Solomon, is supposed to know all about and which he, assisted by two Grand Master-instructed colleagues, whom some would call co-principals, is meant to help us to pursue.

That this is the real answer to the W.M.'s query in the opening ceremony is borne out by some facts that have been there for centuries and yet which no-one has ever seen fit to explain, at least to me. What are these facts?

(1) In the year 1730 there appeared the first exposure of what was claimed to be the current usage in the three degrees as recorded by Samuel Prichard, who described himself as 'a late member of a Constituted Lodge'. Whilst many Masons will be aware of this work, it is also likely that hardly any of them have ever made themselves conversant with its contents. Yet in it are some odd statements which add to the puzzlement over who a Master Mason is or what he should know. Let me explain by quoting from his First Degree and then from the Third Degree:

1° "In the lodge are three great candles, placed on high candlesticks: why so?"
"The sun to rule the day, the moon the night, and the master mason, his Lodge."

3° "If a M.M. you would be, you must understand the rule of 3; And MB [MachBenach] shall make you free; and what you want in Masonry, shall in this Lodge be shown to thee."
"From whence came you?" "From the east."
"Where are you going?" "To the west."
"What are you going to do there?" "To seek for that which WAS lost and is now FOUND."
"What is that which was lost and is now found?" "The M.M. word." "Where was Hiram entertained?" [he surely means 'interred' as later editions state]
"In the Sanctum Sanctorum."
"How was he brought in?" "At the west door of the Temple."

66

"Give me the master's word:"
'Whispers in the ear and supported by the 5 points of fellowship, before mentioned.'

If we were to examine even these extracts in detail it can be appreciated how long that would take but let us at least note that if this is really a correct representation of what was said in ceremonies at this early date then it both agrees but also disagrees with what we are used to. The candidate has pointed out to him the three significant points of the lodge but seems to be given to understand that M.M. and W.M. are the same. If that was true then I repeat one of the previous questions in my earlier book, 'Why are M.Ms excluded when a W.M. is installed?'

Passing on, the candidate moves from east to west to seek for that which was lost. Yet we are now told that what was lost, the M.M.'s true word, is FOUND and to prove that it is found it is whispered along with the F.P.O.F. but it is surely not M.B. that is whispered for as was said earlier, M.B. is the password that makes you free to enter the degree but what is still wanting will be shown. Moreover, this body of Hiram Abi is taken for final burial in the Sanctum Sanctorum through the west door where the veils hung. Yet Jewish law to this day, and our present ritual, state plainly that 'nothing common or unclean was suffered to enter there' and certainly could not be buried in that place. Yet that is where the Free and Accepted Mason is in the end meant to arrive, where the Ark of the Covenant rests. That too is why the Ark of the Covenant appears on our Master Mason's and Royal Arch certificates.

(2) The Freemasonry of the Netherlands took its rise in the 1740s using the practices of the then Grand Lodge in London. In the Third Degree, for example, only 'Machbenach' is used as the word that is conveyed after the exchanging of the F.P.O.F., that being the substituted word that was used by the Modern Freemasons in the 18th century. What might also strike any visitor from England today is that on their tracing board for this degree there is shown on the lid of the coffin an equilateral triangle in the centre of which are the letters YHWH, the Tetragrammaton. This was the name of God which all Jews were forbidden to pronounce, save only the High Priest and then by him only once a year when he entered the Holy of Holies on the Day of Atonement. In the Netherlands this symbol is explained by the Orator who addresses the seated candidate as follows, '...thus M-B became the new Master's Word. Solomon had the OLD Master's Word engraved in a triangle of pure gold and placed in the Holy of Holies.'

(3) And that leads us on to our next fact. If we read the other early Craft exposures produced in France in the 1740s and 1750s we find the following interesting statements in the Third Degree ceremonies. May I point out that these are but three of several more that I could give you.

In 1744: "'What is the name of a Master Mason?
"Harodim or Menatschim."
"What is the name of a master? Adonai Shiloh."
"Give me their meanings? Adonai signifies the Lord; Shiloh signifies his son .
. .'"

67

You should note that there is no mention whatsoever of an MB word, and ADONAI was the usual spoken replacement for YHWH.

In 1747: "'What is the password of a Master [Mason]?" "GIBLOS."
"What was done with the body of our very worthy M?"
"Solomon, to reward his zeal and talents, had him buried in the Sanctuary of the Temple."
"What did he have placed upon the Tomb?"
"A golden medallion, in the shape of a triangle, on which was engraved JEHOVAH, the former word of a Master, which is the name of God in Hebrew.'"

In 1751 [in the address given by the Lodge Orator]:
"'Today you make your way into the heart of the Sanctuary; the veil that covered it is drawn back so that you may see it. Cast your eyes on the design drawn by the hand of the artist, the representation of the tomb that the wisest of Monarchs erected over the Worthy Master whose memory we celebrate . . .
"You notice a Hebrew name whose significance should be known to you. It was formerly reserved for the Masters of the ancient lodge, but ignorance of what occurred at the tragic end of Lord Hiram [Adoniram] prevented the brethren from preserving it after his death, and they preferred to bury it with him, rather than expose themselves to the risk of using a word that might then become known to fellows . . .'"

I must just comment here that again an MB word is missing and it may be noted that at this stage of ritual development the symbol that still appears on the Dutch boards is amply explained as a natural part of the Third Degree.

(4) And that naturally leads us to the fourth fact. On many Third Degree tracing boards in England there appear scenes on the coffin. These show the doorway of the Holy of Holies with the veils drawn back and the Ark of the Covenant standing beyond. No one in my 54 years' experience has ever said more about why such a scene is displayed than that it is where the High Priest went once a year on the Day of Atonement. What now seems clear is that we have at last a much more satisfactory reason for these scenes being there. It is the goal of a true Master Mason, NOT a substituted one, and there, in the most holy part of the Temple the lost secrets of the Free and Accepted Craft are found. Today it is as a Royal Arch Mason that you know the answer and that surely means that that is where the M.M. degree is quite clearly meant to be completed. We have moved from the East to the West to discover the true secret where the full truth of the Deity is revealed.

I now want to pass, however, to another puzzle connected with this degree and that has again only recently caught my attention. I refer to the Password associated with this degree. Why ever is it Tubalcain? Just what has that to do with the main import of what we are about in this ceremony? It is not at all clear when you contrast its use with what has gone before. To use the words 'Free and of good report' for a E.A. is most apt as relating to the grounds on which we are admitted. In the explanation of the Second Degree tracing board the word Shibboleth is demonstrated as fitting for those who seek

69

that step. Is Tubalcain used in the Third Degree because he was the 'first artificer in metals' and Hiram Abi supervised the casting of the two great pillars? But if we are talking about Boaz and Jakin then surely the First or Second Degree would be more apt for the use of T.C.? And would you believe that in a 1751 French exposure, entitled 'The Mason Unmasked', we read the following passage? 'What are the Passwords? TUBALCAIN for the Apprentice; SHIBBOULETH for the Fellow; and GIBLIM for the Master [Mason].'

Don't you find that interesting? Apparently our forebears thought about these matters more carefully than we seem to have done and they came up with this very fitting choice. Why was the change made? Could it be that when part of the Third Degree was to be reserved for those who were Installed, or Past, Masters they needed a special Password and to fill the gap that was then left the one for the Apprentice was given to the Third Degree? I am only speculating but then with such a puzzling degree that is what Masons who think have to do.

Another feature that has made me stop and think is the marked difference between the items that are displayed on our present Third Degree tracing board and those of some remaining Boards in England (Bath) and Wales (Llandudno) and the normal display in Scotland. Noticeable among the items are the pots of manna and of incense and the Rod of Aaron and I was reminded of the introduction in one of Dr. George Oliver's books in 1847 where he wrote:

'Several Masonic emblems which were formerly attached to the Third Degree are disposed in order [he meant an old Royal Arch floorcloth] viz, the golden candlestick, the table of shewbread, the pot of manna and of incense ... all of which confirms my opinion regarding the transfer of the latter portions of the Third Degree to the Royal Arch.' This at least is a help in solving one puzzle.

I turn to yet another of the puzzles for today. It is widely believed, and we are always told, that this degree took its rise in the mid-1720s after it had been used irregularly for admitting members to the Philo-Musicae Society. I have to admit that I always found this a trifle odd because there was never any explanation of where that Society got it from. There has naturally been much speculation as to how and from where such a degree emerged. One fact, however, seems to have been frequently overlooked. Let me explain.

In 1717 there was the need for new oversight of certain lodges in the London and Westminster area. We now know from a work just published in Holland why Sir Christopher Wren had resigned from the post of Grand Master Mason in 1711 and consequently a new oversight and leadership in London was required. Four of the lodges decided to elect one of their members to fill the post and a bookseller, Bro Anthony Sayer, was chosen. His main qualification for the position was that he was 'the oldest [i.e. the most senior] Master Mason among them'.

Doesn't this ring a curious bell? We know that Sayer was clearly not a working Master Mason of the stonemasons' trade and the degree of a Free and accepted Master Mason is not supposed to have been available until almost a decade later. How could this brother bookseller then be 'the most senior Master Mason'? The only answer that is possible is that some form of M.M. degree must already have been known and practised by Free and Accepted Freemasons before 1726 and even before 1716.

To our aid again at this point comes the same book by Dr Oliver that I referred to

aware of the auspices under which they gather — and have gathered for a century and more?

Those, I suggest, are perfectly proper questions for people to put to us, or to put to one another out of our hearing, especially now that the general public has access to these rooms, however infrequently.

Yet even more importantly we ought to be asking these questions of ourselves. How can I, a professed member of a religious body that follows the teaching of Scripture which frowns on witchcraft and the wrongly occult teaching of a pagan society, bear to meet in such a setting and still hope to set an example for others to follow? Each of us doubtless could imagine similar doubts and queries that might arise in our minds as we begin to reflect on having a zodiac permanently in our midst.

If I am right and those really are fair comments by others or within ourselves then what do we do to start dealing with them? It seems to me that there are three things we have to do. First we have to understand properly just what the zodiac is. Second, we have to understand why it has a place in Freemasonry; and third, we need to know in particular why it is here at Duncombe Place. It is to those issues that I now want to turn.

The zodiac didn't just happen. A recent book by a friend of mine deals with the whole growth of the study of the heavens in the days of the Babylonian and Assyrian Empires. Let me quote one or two sentences. 'Detailed analysis of the astrological tablets in the library at Nineveh quickly revealed two important facts: first, that astrology developed over a long period of time . . . and second that the astrology found in these tablets was not concerned with the fate of individuals [i.e. horoscopes] but with the affairs of society. Moreover the zodiacal signs are absent.' In other words to equate astrology and the zodiac is not correct. How then did the concept of the zodiac arise? Let me try to explain.

So that the rulers of the early Middle Eastern kingdoms could rule effectively they needed an accurate calendar. The first astrologers sought to provide this by literally 'watching the stars' and reading what they saw, which is why they have the name *astero-logoi* (astrologers). Yet in the Middle East, sandstorms, dust clouds and even sometimes rain clouds might conceal the stars at just the moments that mattered most. So they had to think of a further way of getting the information that would enable them to give the kings what they needed. They had to acquire an understanding of the regular movements of the Sun and Moon across the heavens so that even if those important planets were obscured their position in the sky could be ascertained. That meant working out mathematical 'paths' for those major stars and setting those cyclical movements down as reliable 'laws'. That is why these 'wise men' now became not only 'star-gazers' but star-lawyers or *astero-nomoi* (astronomers). It is in connection with their efforts to discover these Sun- and Moon-paths, regardless of whether they could be physically seen, that we come to the formulation of the zodiac. The zodiac was part of the process involved in trying to establish a plan of the heavens on which to base calculations.

How did that work? Despite their still fairly primitive time-keeping, these star-gazers eventually arranged the star-clusters or constellations into four groups and recorded them on tablets which later became instruments called 'star-takers' or *astero-labes* (astrolabes). Originally these were circular tables divided into 12 segments with three concentric circles, and in the 36 spaces thus provided they placed a separate star and gave it a number. Before too long they had deduced that these numbers related to the length of a day and then other calculations followed. Eventually they worked out that the Moon passed through a belt 12 degrees wide and the Sun and other planets also moved in this same 'path' — the Ancients' *Star Trek*.

The 36 divisions were first reduced to 18 and finally to 12 and it was then that these 12 stable and basic guides to the movement of the heavenly bodies — the foundation of modern astronomy — were given names. Tablets began to record the zodiacal placing of the important planets and anyone who wishes to do so can see the largest collection of these in our own British Museum. The zodiac marks the entry into astrology and astronomy of mathematics and calculation. Its use by the ancients for birth-charts was a by-product. Its main contribution was as a more precise method of describing the heavens at any given time and that, by any standard, was a step in pure science. The astrologers had gained a much greater understanding of the celestial cycles upon which a reliable calendar of the year could be based.

If that helps to explain how the idea of the zodiac came into being and where it was initially meant to assist the life of society, it still does not explain why the name and its various components were selected. Let us now try to understand both of these elements.

The name is of course derived from the Greek language and thus reveals that the zodiac, as we are accustomed to view it, arose when the Greek scholars began to interest themselves in Babylonian astrology. We know, for example, that Pythagoras first went to study in Egypt but was captured by the Persians, who had in turn also conquered Babylon and Assyria. Indeed it was whilst Pythagoras was in Babylon that he was taught by a famous Zoroastrian scholar and finally composed his great work on 'The Musical Harmony of the Universe'. Pythagoras would have known all about the zodiac.

The word 'zoo' is familiar to us all, even if it is not as popular today as it certainly was 50 years ago. The word means 'a place where living creatures exist', for *zoe* is the Greek word for 'life'. From that word we get *zoidiakos* which means 'creature-like' or 'animal-like' and hence the Latin word *zodiacus* which gave us the English word. Yet the Greek word *zoidiakos* was an adjective and needs a noun to go with it. The whole phrase was really *kuklon zoidiakon* which means 'a circle of living creatures' and that of course exactly describes what is on the ceiling over our heads. It is a band or path of very active human or animal-like creatures moving round in a circular fashion, hence *progression*. It is this feature that can still be seen drawn round the celestial globe that adorns many an ancient lodge room, or even on a small globe that sometimes caps the pillar on the Junior Warden's pedestal. The presence of the zodiac in Freemasonry is still as alive as the figures that comprise it. It has a rightly honoured place in our Old York traditions.

Before we come to that, however, we must tackle the matter of why the figures of the zodiac are the ones that they are. With so scientific an origin it is to be expected that they are not there by whim or chance. The answer as far as the names and various figures is concerned is really quite simple. The titles we give them today are those that were applied to them by the Greeks who kept only five of the original Babylonian names. The reason for this difference is again very simple when you remember that looking at the night sky from around the Aegean Sea is different from looking at it from the area of the Persian Gulf — at least if you are using only your ordinary eyesight. The original descriptions were those as seen from Babylon and the more clinical and precise Greek 'star-gazers' decided that other shapes, especially related to their own myths and legends, were appropriate.

Moreover, it was the Greeks who later discovered that even the constellations changed their positions over time and that this accounted for differing views of them. The final and most decisive change in any appreciation of the zodiac came, of course, with the discovery of the telescope by Galileo, when the hitherto comparatively simple sky-pattern was peopled with a great new influx of previously unknown bodies. It was then that astronomy began to diverge from astrology.

Why the figures of the zodiac came in the order that they did was because that is how the Babylonians first saw them appear through the year. What was later discerned and considered as important by the early speculative Freemasons was that the creatures represented in turn the elements of fire, earth, air and water, four times over. It was this kind of knowledge, as well as their ancient connection with the succession of the seasons and their importance to the first calendar and clock makers, that ensured constant Masonic interest in the zodiac. It had nothing to do with natal charts or horoscopes. The connection of Freemasonry with this 'ancient scientific aid' was on another plane.

This is seen by two quotations that I now want to share with you. The first is found in Richard Carlile's *Manual of Freemasonry* that was first produced about 1823. In addition to the extensive rituals of the period which he reproduced, he also wrote some commentaries on what he regarded as the pros and cons of the Masonic contribution to Man's well-being. For him the most valuable of all human virtues was Truth. At one stage he wrote this:

'But for planetary motion, there could have been no division of time. The relations of the sun to the planets and fixed stars, make up all the natural divisions of time; such as the day, the month, the year, and the corresponding seasons. The day is marked by the motion of the earth on its own axis. The month [the lunar measurement] by the appearances of the moon; and the calendar [the solar or sun's measurement] by the grouping of the stars into twelve divisions, which are called the Zodiac.'

Make no mistake. Whilst there were some aspects of our Fraternity that Carlile criticised, having the zodiac in our halls was not one of them. For him that was a mark of the truth of things.

The other quotation will, I hope, be of even more interest and perhaps surprise. During the last two years a very determined effort by one of the Freemasons in Newcastle upon Tyne has led to the complete re-ordering and refurbishment of the Provincial Library at Neville Hall in that city. As a result of many hours happy research there, I have been able to lay my hands on the earliest extant versions of the Harodim working that was prevalent in that area between about 1730 and 1800. What is important for us is that it is strongly believed that much of that working either derived from or was paralleled by Old York working. What I am therefore going to read to you might in the same or some similar form have actually have been given in this city and alongside the emblem that is over our heads tonight. It is an Astronomical Lecture applicable to Master Masons. (Let me hasten to add that that does not apply to Master Masons today.) Here it is, or at least part of it, for the whole would take about 20 minutes to deliver.

'Q: How many of the 12 signs of the Zodiac are peculiarly applicable to our valuable secrets in the M.M. degree?

A: Seven: viz. Castor and Pollux [or Gemini], Leo [or the Lion], Virgo [or the Virgin Astrea], Libra [or the Scales], Capricorn [or the Goat], Pisces [or the Fish] and Apelles [the Painter].

Q: Please to explain them?

A: Castor and Pollux loved each other so tenderly that they never were asunder . . . . a true emblem of brotherly love; and as such used to be drawn on the Apron of every newly initiated Brother. This act of fraternal affection occasioned their being metamorphosed and turned into stars and made a constellation . . . being the lively images of the twins belonging to our G.M.H.Ab . . .

       Leo: in the reign of King Solomon a Lion ran through the streets of Jerusalem spreading everywhere the utmost terror and dismay. The wife of Solomon's chief Architect, with her infant in her arms, dropped it in her fright when it was immediately seized upon by the Lion . . . she threw herself upon her knees before the animal and implored with all the energy and expression of a Mother in despair. The Lion stopped, fixed his eyes upon her, placed the infant unharmed on the ground and departed . . .

       Virgo: she is represented as a virgin with a stern and majestic countenance holding a pair of scales in one hand and a sword in the other.'

Brethren, I will not quote more for fear of wearying you, but now I trust you can look up with confidence to what is above your heads and hold your heads up high. The zodiac is a rightful part of our heritage.

(For anyone who wishes to know still more about the zodiac in Freemasonry, the author has copies of his Batham lecture, 'The Path of the Zodiac in Freemasonry', which is available on application to him.)

SURPRISES IN SCOTTISH LODGES

It would not be a surprise at all if, as a result of the many visits that I have already made in these last few years to hundreds of Masonic halls in England and Wales, I did not find that there was 'little new under the sun' and this might even have been expected in the ancient and noble realm of Scotland. As one friend said to me, 'Surely the mine of discovery is at last running out and you are going to be hard put to it to find seams of worthwhile material in future visits?' The answer in this case, after three long visits in three separate periods to the Craft lodge rooms and Royal Arch Chapter meeting places of Scotland, is that I never cease to be surprised by things unusual and unique, and often when one least expects them. If I can interest you on this occasion by preparing you for some of the treasures that will appear in full in the books still to be published and revealing our Northern Masonic Kingdom then I will be satisfied.

My first surprise was soon borne in upon me when, during my first tour, I found three halls *all* claiming to be the oldest continuously-used ones in the country. I had expected, and found, that there were still smoldering embers of the fiery debate as to which was the oldest *lodge* in Scotland — that is, between Kilwinning, Edinburgh, Melrose and Aberdeen — but the claims for the oldest *premises* did jolt me. It even gave me problems about the possible contents page of my book and I hope that what I might provide will, with the close cooperation of the then Grand Secretary in Edinburgh, smooth all hackles. We English, after all, have to be careful when treading on such hallowed ground.

I intend therefore to speak briefly at the outset about these four contending parties and their lodge rooms, and then take you on a scattered trip to six others. That, I am sure, will surprise you enough.

I begin with Lodge No 0 (Yes, number zero) just to the north of Ayr. To find oneself at last in front of the red sandstone building that houses this ancient lodge is itself a surprise, and not least when you read the words across the facade: 'Mother Lodge Kilwinning'. Not a banner but carved in stone. To stand then, in its richly endowed museum, to try on one of the members' famous Kilwinning aprons that are still in use and which have no emblems or decoration whatsoever (as in operative days) and then to stand at the pedestal that is used for the obligations, and is almost in the centre of the floor, is to have more surprises. On the top of the present pedestal (quite separate from the Master's or, as they say, Right Worshipful Master's, desk) is an engraved plaque. It reads, in translation from the Latin words it bears: 'Under the leadership and guidance of Archibald, the Rt. Hon. the Earl of Eglinton, and his deputy, John Allen, etc. etc., the ancient Mother Lodge of Kilwinning was rebuilt. The Foundation stone was laid 24 March 1779 in the Masonic Year 5779.' You will notice '*re*built'.

Here, you suddenly discover, is where a recent former Assistant Grand Master of England stood when he was initiated by his father, the previous Earl of Eglinton. Their estate, not surprisingly, is not very far away. Here too stood the young man, earlier than them both, who organised the famous, or disastrous, Eglinton Tournament in 1839.

The Lodge of Edinburgh (Mary's Chapel) No 1 is unswerving in its claim to be the premier lodge of all Scotland. Its premises within are very distinctive but it has an unpretentious external face in a rear street that runs parallel with the renowned George Street, where stand the headquarters of the Grand Lodge of Scotland itself. We are here in what is still called the 'New Town' of Edinburgh though it was built in the 18th century.

The claim of this 'ludge' is so strong that it is written in Scottish native script on the ceiling of their old meeting place at the top of the building. The extract in question is from the Schaw Statutes of 1598 which were happily rediscovered in 1859 after a long and hidden existence in — of all places, would you believe — the archives of the Earls of Eglinton. In part they state:

'1598   The Statutes and observances to be obeyed by all the master masons within this realm.
1599   Edinburgh shall be in all times coming as of before the first and principal ludge of Scotland.'

The minute books of this lodge are still complete from 1599, which makes the celebrations of the Grand Lodge of England over 275 years seem quite jejune. I find it still very moving in this hall when, at the close of a lodge meeting, the Right Worshipful Master and his Worshipful Wardens move from their chairs to the floor of the lodge and all present form a rough circle, so that the lodge may literally be closed 'on the level with all true brethren'. Having closed all too briefly here, we must turn south again.

The Melrose Hall belongs to the Lodge of Melrose St John No 12 (or No 1*bis*), which means 'equal to and twinning Lodge No 1'. The ancestry here is of minutes from 1594 continuously and a tradition that there has been an operative lodge here since 1136, founded to build the Abbey of Melrose for King David — of Scotland, of course. Two surprises here are the fact that this lodge parades publicly every St John's Day, whatever the winter weather, with a band to lead their flag and the officers of the lodge, the latter all duly clothed and carrying their Right Worshipful Master's and Worshipful Wardens' batons, their Bible (a Geneva or 'Breeches' Bible, of course) and all wearing hats. They process three times round the Market Cross close to their hall and then head off for the Abbey grounds where they thread their way through the ruins, assisted by the letting off of fireworks and with pitch torches blazing, before they return to the hall for the closing of the lodge and some well-earned warming refreshment.

Nearly a century ago the *Southern Reporter* stated: 'The proceedings were somewhat marred by the heavy rain and some senseless cracking of squibs prevented the bulk of the people from hearing the remarks of the Grand Master.' In case you think that this latter gentleman was a visitor for the occasion from Edinburgh or London, let me surprise you by explaining that until 1891 this lodge acted as a Grand Lodge which chartered other new lodges, especially south of the Clyde. It thus had a presiding officer called 'The Grand Master' and not just Right Worshipful Master.

The other surprise, though by no means the last, is the presence on the walls of the upstairs lodge room of a framed document entitled 'A Panegyric upon the Excellent Art of Masons' by James Donaldson. It was written in 1711 and was gifted to the lodge by Bro John Mein in 1721. A few of its sentiments are worth recording here:

'Another thing they have all Arts do lack,
In which no other with them doth partake;
Namely that house to which the Tribes did go,
To sacrifice and pray in Times of old,
As by the Sacred Scriptures we are told,
Figur'd the Temple of this Glorious One,
Who is himself called the Chief Corner Stone,
And sure Foundation of the Spiritual Dome
Of living Stones together join'd, in whom
They're knit together in one Frame Compleat,
In him they rest, in him they all do meet.'

In Aberdeen we come to the ancient lodge of that city which has the number 13 (or 1*ter*), which means 'equal to No 1 but the third partner'. To enter their Hall after admiring the superb granite facade — and it is, after all, called 'The Granite City' — is immediately to have a surprise. There in front of you is a huge horizontal 12-foot-diameter representation of the zodiac in full coloured marble inlay. The effect is stunning, and then you also notice that at the edges of the chequered flooring around this circle the corners all contain not tassels or squares and compasses but triple taus. Though I cannot go into this matter in a Craft lodge I should tell the Royal Arch Companions present that these two forms, the zodiac and the triple tau, have very close linkage in those Scottish chapters that lie outside the district between Scotland and England known as the Borders.

You then lift your eyes from the floor and see before you a massive Austrian oak fireplace with an overmantel that reaches up to the ceiling, some 20 feet from the ground. Above the marble surround of the iron grate are four rectangular panels that bear words in the ancient Doric speech or dialect of this land of Scotland. They read: SEN VORD IS THRALL / AND THOCHT IS FRE / KEIP VEILL THY TONGE / I CONSEILL THEE, which may be roughly translated: 'Since your word is given and your mind is free, keep watch over your tongue is my advice to thee.'

There is another vast surprise in this hall for those who are Royal Arch Masons, but this is not the place for this underground feature to be described adequately, even though I have been fortunate in being given permission for the first time to describe such Royal Arch items. Any forthcoming books will be the place for this to be explained and fully illustrated.

I pass next to the Lodge Dalkeith Kilwinning No 10. This lodge, too, is very insistent on its having the most ancient continuity in its meeting place. Its hall is certainly a most fascinating building, with ancient Masons Marks repositioned on its passage ceilings by modern decorators. In the temple there is a huge white stone statue of St Andrew, showing him spread-eagled on his cross and dominating the north wall. Yet the most surprising feature of this hall is the fact that the Senior Warden sits in a chair that is almost a third of the way down the room from the west wall. There are even six rows of chairs behind him. When I asked why he was not nearer to the present entrance of the temple in the west, the answer given was:

'Ah, but you see his chair is where it has always been since this hall was built. A century ago we took down the old west wall that was right behind him, and to make more space we incorporated the room that was behind that wall. This gave us what we wanted but the Warden has always sat there and there he stays.'

A further surprise in the hall is that in the south and north walls, on a level with the Senior Warden's chair, there are two niches painted brown and standing about 2ft 6in from the ground. These were first placed in the corners of the original temple and alongside the doorways that then existed. Their possible use puzzled me until I suddenly realised what was later confirmed, that they were 'aids to comfort' for the dining and drinking brethren in the lodge room. They were able to make use of them without having to disturb the Tyler and seek permission to leave. That I must confess, was a feature I had never seen before.

In the showcase of this temple is a magnificent Tyler's outfit that looks good enough to have served one of the Monarch's Regiments of Foot. It is bright red, with a distinctive sash, a cocked hat and cloak. One is usually prepared for a more sombre type of clothing for this officer and the surprise is therefore all the greater. Yet this is not the only such striking Tyler's outfit in this northern kingdom. Outside the entrance passage that leads to the main temple of the no less ancient Lodge of Scone and Perth, in the latter town, you will find a life-size model of the ancient Tyler there and he is clothed in a white turban, blue velvet overjacket and baggy white trousers, with shoes having upturned toes. He clearly represents the person shown in a nearby portrait, the actual Tyler of this lodge in days past. Having given him at least a knowing look, you pass into their breath-taking temple, a description of which in full you must look for elsewhere.

Let me simply tell you that at the centre of the room is a circular altar with a small side basin in which is lit a certain 'glimmering ray' for all the three degrees. We have been at such a central obligation pedestal in Kilwinning but what you see here, on one of the many painted murals round the walls, is a scene of King James VI of Scotland (and I of England) being initiated in this very lodge and holding out his hand over the flame that rises from this very pedestal, albeit in an earlier hall than this one. The continuity and real link with Royalty in the Craft together with the drama of such a scene all combine to create a real moment of surprise that I am sure you can appreciate.

Another lodge at Newburgh in Fife — Lodge Lindores No 106 — was not as careful about its possessions as those I have just mentioned. It was my turn to administer a surprise to my hosts. In the anteroom of the temple I noticed a portrait of yet another old Tyler in the mid-19th century. He was dressed in the ancient garb provided for him by this country town lodge. 'We thought you would find that picture of interest', they said, 'but sadly the clothing was lost and we therefore treasure this picture.' I too regretted not seeing another distinctive local Tyler's get-up. So we turned to the items that did remain in the lodge room — one of which again could take your breath away but must await revelation in my books — and I eventually noticed a white, glass fronted cupboard set into the north wall.

'What is in there?' I enquired.

'Nothing but junk which we have never really sorted out,' was the answer.

Could we see it, I wondered, for I have heard those words so often before. They unlocked the glass doors and there was junk. What there also was amongst the rubbish was a bundle of clothing. We unwrapped it and lo, to their complete surprise and my delight, we had discovered the blue and yellow stockings, the blue and silver-edged waistcoat and the light overjacket of the Tyler we had seen portrayed. The hat and outside coat had gone but I have helped one more lodge to treasure its past afresh and its possessions more carefully.

There remain three more surprises that I would like to share with you before I finish. They all have to do with helping to teach about the Craft degrees that we carry out.

The first is a board of large proportions that was given to the Lodge of Greenock St John's No 175, on the Clyde's south bank, at the time of the lodge's inception in 1791. It has hung on their walls since that time and reveals on its much illustrated surface all the tools of the three degrees and even some symbols of the Royal Arch. Why this board was both provided and used was as follows.

Because Greenock was a seaport that flourished, many seamen and merchants from the Continent came into Masonry through this lodge. Yet because their stay locally might be quite brief, they were given the three degrees in one evening. Yes, that does probably surprise you. Hence they needed a board that would serve their purpose. In addition, if they could come back the next month (or later) after being made a Master Mason they could be 'exalted' into the Royal Arch in the same lodge and they used the same board.

This persisted as their practice until 1868, when the Grand Lodge of Scotland asked them to stop giving the three degrees at one time. They refused, on the grounds that this was what they had always done. Two years later, however, a new view had prevailed and someone presented them with three separate boards, as they had promised not to do more than *two* degrees for one candidate in any one evening. One Past Master then said that perhaps they could now do the work 'in full', which suggests how they had done the three previously. What is still interesting is that because the symbols of the degrees have always appeared in the lodge room all the time it has existed, the new boards are never covered up, whatever degree is being worked.

In Musselburgh we come to the fine old Lodge at Fisherrow, close by the oldest golf links in the country. The lodge actually still meets in part of what was the original Golf House that the Masons bought. I was told here that there were NO tracing boards and there never have been any. How could that be, I wondered. The Secretary, who showed me around the building, also demonstrated the answer to this puzzle. He acted out, for my benefit, the whole of their Third Degree ceremony which is learnt by heart *without books*.

They also have their own form of the ritual and at the end of the 'raising' they display all the items for the teaching of the degree on the steps below the RW Master's place. Those who have seen the oldest Third Degree tracing boards that I have shown in the halls at Bath and at Llandudno (North Wales) will now see in Musselburgh all that the former only have drawn as pictures — the coffin, skull and crossbones, the Ark of Noah, the incense and manna jars, the scythe, the sword pointing to the heart, the beehive and the heavy maul, the plumb, the level and the hour glass. They are here very powerful visual aids and the instructing Past Master, like this admirable Secretary, can actually lift the items and present them to the candidate so that he remembers them. That was a real surprise and the surprise was continued when I was able to tell the people in Llandudno that the explanation of all the items they have, but the meaning of which they had lost, could now be supplied by asking a brother from Musselburgh to pay them a visit.

Finally, I take you to Dunbartonshire, north of the Clyde. In a few lodges there they use one of the most remarkable rituals in all English-speaking Freemasonry. It is called the John McBride working and it is totally different in presentation to anything that most other British Masons know. It too has no tracing boards.

It is principally worked in full in the hall at Renton, where John McBride was a member and where the hall was specifically built for his working. You therefore see two enormous pillars, some 25 feet high, at the west end of the temple, and behind and through them the winding stair of three, five and seven steps leads to a real middle chamber through the Veils of the upper temple. There, against the light from behind the candidate, the brethren below hear the lecture of *their* Second Degree delivered to the new Fellow of the Craft. Needless to say, at both the foot and top of the staircase he has been actually challenged for a password. For the remainder of this remarkable building you will again have to read what I trust will eventually be produced — but that, I am certain, is by now no surprise at all.

May I say that I hope that this short pilgrimage will reveal the ongoing search that we can all make in learning about this great Craft of ours. We can in truth take real steps to make those daily advancements in Masonic knowledge which were urged upon us at the outset of our journey.

HUGUENOT FREEMASONS

(The Huguenot Lodge in London invited me to write this paper some years ago, commemorating the 300th Anniversary of the Huguenot community in England.) Providentially, but unintentionally, I found myself six days ago in the border country of Languedoc and Provence, to be specific, in the city of Nîmes and the town of Uzès. As I wandered down their ancient streets and gazed upon their attractive house facades, I naturally allowed my mind to turn afresh to this address which I had prepared to deliver to you on my return. To see also that sun-baked countryside, with its trim vineyards and red-roofed white-walled villages, and to see those mountain valleys which had been the homeland of so many Huguenots who came seeking refuge here after the revocation of the Edict of Nantes in 1685, only served to underline for me the depth of their longing for freedom and their eagerness for a security which their own nation could not offer them.

In one sense it is sad to think of how great a treasure was lost to France by the emigration of such a people — though that sadness cannot but be tinged with an ironic delight at how England benefited from all that these newcomers were able to offer in their new homeland: tapestry making in Exeter, silk and cotton manufacture in Bideford, sail-making in Ipswich, papermaking in Southampton, hat-styling in Wandsworth and language teaching in Cheam. And that is but a random selection from the range of skills that these scholars and craftsmen, whether employers or employed, were able to share with the English. And it is in one Craft in particular that we should be particularly interested this evening to hear of their involvement. For make no mistake, the place of the Huguenot male citizen of the early 18th century in the development and establishing of the English Grand Lodge was notable and extensive.

My mind was first drawn to this subject in a fresh way as I read that latest contribution to English Huguenot history, Robin Gwynn's book, *Huguenot Heritage*. On page 90, appropriately at the end of a chapter entitled 'Professions', the author unpretentiously points out that the very first Grand Steward after the formation of the Grand Lodge in 1717 was Josiah Villeneau, a refugee, who went on to become Senior Grand Warden in 1721. In 1725 we find the Walloon protestant, John James Heidegger, wearing the same red apron and then, in a quite continuous stream after the revival of the Stewards' Lodge in 1730, there are one or more Huguenot members every year:

1730   Ezekiel Varenne
1731   Thomas Durant and George Fage
1732   Claude Crespigny (and Solomon Mendes)
1733   John Pollexfen and Dr John Mizaubin
1734   Isaac Meure
1735   Dr Meyer Schomberg

and the list goes on: Barrett, Beaumont, Bernard, Carne, Caton, Combrune, De Charmes, De Vaux, Faber, Foy, Hemet, Le Bas, Le Maistre, Ruck and Vol.

Suddenly you find yourself immersed in a whole new dimension of allegiance to the Masonic Order by these fresh citizens of the realm and as you read through Colin Dyer's fascinating account of the Grand Stewards' Lodge, published in 1985, you will be made to see how the strain persists to this very day, with Pierrepont and Cazenove appointed in 1985 and a former Deputy Grand Master, the Hon Edward Latham Baillieu. To pursue further that channel of Masonic history would be enough for this evening if we were wanting to exhaust the whole range of our subject. Let me at least add that no less than one quarter of all the recorded Stewards' names in Grand Lodge are those of recognisable Huguenot origin — but what of those whose names have, or had soon, become totally anglicised?

Let us however turn to another source of interest for the Huguenot Mason. In her book, *They came as Strangers* (1959), Francesca Wilson reminds us that these Huguenot refugees introduced the art of calico-printing and wax-bleaching, the weaving of velvet, silk stockings, gauze, table-linen, etc. 'They brought with them new ways of manufacturing ribbons, tapestry, baize . . . new modes of dyeing and of making hats and looking-glasses. The first person who contrived a machine moved by steam was Savary, and the best maker of telescopes was Dollond . . .' (p. 27)

In 1934 Bro F. W. Golby took up this inventiveness as a scope for Masonic research and published a paper in *AQC* entitled, 'Our early brethren as Patentees'. You will not be surprised to learn something of what he found in that study. There is James Christopher Le Blon/Blun who patented the 'Multiplying of Pictures' on 5 February 1719, and in 1730 his name duly appears in the list of the lodge at the Crown and Sceptre in St Martin's Lane. There is John Martin, Doctor, Fellow of the Royal Society in 1727, who patented on 7 May 1720 a method of 'Meliorating oils'. He is recorded in the 1725 list as one of the Wardens of the lodge meeting at the Golden Lion in Dean Street. Daniel Niblet, coppersmith, and William Vreen, instrument maker, are two more brethren who patented 'Heating by steam for various manufacturing processes' in 1720, whilst in July 1721 John Senex joins with two Englishmen, Harris and Wilson, to patent the making of 'Globular charts'. Senex appears in the 1725 list of the lodge meeting at the Fleece in Fleet Street. Bro Thomas Chanifleur is perhaps someone whom whisky- and other drinkers may have very good cause to remember with gratitude, for he patented 'a water syphon' on 15 April 1724.

John Senex, who was mentioned above, subsequently became Grand Warden and also a Fellow of the Royal Society in 1728. He was proposed to that important position by no less a person than Dr Halley — of whose comet we are constantly reminded (and which I must tell you I saw in the Canaries when last it appeared) — and recommended as a Fellow by the President. To qualify, Senex had 'presented his draughts of the Constellations laid down from Mr. Flamsteed's Catalogue containing the Northern and Southern hemispheres in two sheets with the constellations in the Zodiac . . . and he also showed the Society his two new large Globes of 28in diameter'. I think you will agree, considering the pillars of which we are taught, that was an appropriate thing for a Masonic Fellow of the Royal Society to produce.

Indeed one of the factors in 18th as well as late 17th century Masonry was the surprisingly close connection between the Royal Society and the Craft. On 4 July 1728, we read that John Senex 'gave his Bond, signed his obligation and was admitted a Fellow'. You might be forgiven for thinking that that referred to the second degree of Freemasonry but you would be wrong. That was his admittance, like so many other Huguenot brethren, into the Royal Society. Incidentally, it is worth remembering that at the date 1728 we have no evidence to suggest that there was anything more for a Freemason to do than become a 'Fellow' in speculative Freemasonry, for it was only with Prichard's exposure in 1730 that we have any indication of the content of the Third Degree. The parallel with Craft and Royal Society practice is, or was then, very much closer than it might now seem.

Senex, however, was not alone. Bro J. R. Clarke tells us in his illuminating article, 'The Royal Society and Early Grand Lodge Freemasonry' (*AQC* vol 80, pp. 110ff) that from its inception in 1662, as part of the Stuart Restoration, the Society 'numbered amongst its Fellows some of the most inquiring minds of the age; they were curious about everything and some of them — Ashmole, Aubrey, Locke and Wren — had shown themselves to be inquisitive about Masonry . . .' He goes on (p. 111): 'A preliminary survey [shows] that nearly all the noble Grand Masters during the first 50 years of the existence of Grand Lodge were Fellows of the Royal Society, and that their Deputies during the first ten years had the same honour . . .' For our present purpose it is enough to notice from the 1723–1730 lists the following refugee Masons who were also in the Society: Clare, De la Faye, De Loraine, Du Bois, Dugood, Folkes, Hody, Machin, Papillon, Rutty and Schomberg.

From that list I have, as with several previous references, left out one of the most distinguished early Freemasons of all, John Theophilus Desaguliers. He was also a proposer of Senex as a Fellow of the Society, being one himself, and he it was who caused the revival of the Grand Stewards' Lodge in 1728 when he was again Deputy Grand Master, having been Grand Master 1719/20. It was Desaguliers who was a co-patentee with Niblet and Vreen in their 'Steam processing' just as he was a patentee in his own right in regard to 'water systems' — a subject which drew him in a professional capacity all over these islands and even led to his being given the freedom of Dunfermline. He is the very epitome of the early 18th-century Huguenot Freemason, born at La Rochelle in 1683 as the son of a Pastor at Aitre, and himself becoming a parson of the Church of England, though 'somewhile pastor of the French Chapel in Swallow Street'. He married Margaret Thomas La Chapelle in France and I have to claim a very special interest in him because he was a student at Oxford in the very same college as myself, Hart Hall, that is now known as Hertford College.

It is in Desaguliers that we find all those characteristics that both bring distinction to the Huguenot contribution to this land and such great credit to the émigré company of which he was a part. We see his scholarship honoured by the Royal Society, in his being awarded the Copley Gold Medal in acknowledgment of his continuing experiments (at the age of 60) in bridge construction, water supplies and steam control. Perhaps those may seem odd matters for a clergyman to engage in but they simply reveal those great Huguenot traits of inventiveness and dedication. When we also recognise his wholesale devotion to the Masonic Order, his leadership there and his assistance to Dr Anderson in compiling those first Grand Constitutions that preserve tolerance in religion and freedom from any political bias, we again note the Huguenot characteristics. It was no part of these new Englishmen to return to the evil experiences of their mother country. To be part of a movement such as ours where a Free man of full age could associate naturally with all other adult men in an atmosphere of mutual concord and fraternal affection was an answer to all their prayers. From the persecution of Rome, from the brutality of political dragooning, and from the fear of not being able to practise their daily avocation, these men found in Freemasonry a code and a manner of life that they could truly cherish.

Above all else, they could in their Masonry express the new-found loyalty to a royal house that was also part of their scriptural upbringing. Desaguliers was chaplain to the Duke of Chandos; he was asked to demonstrate his experiments before George II, who admired him greatly, and in 1727 he was appointed chaplain to Frederick, Prince of Wales. He was a favourite of Queen Caroline and in 1738 was Chaplain to the Bowes (later 12th) Regiment of Dragoons — an ironic twist of fate, since it was this brand of French soldiery that had led to his flight, as some say, on board ship in a barrel. Those who want to pursue this great man's fuller career should read Bro John Stokes's essay in *AQC* vol 38 (1925) where almost every known detail of the Masonic and secular career of Desaguliers is recorded.

Yet it would be wrong to stop with this well-known Huguenot Mason. We need to record that his assistant in his experimental laboratory was another Huguenot Mason, Charles Labelye, himself the engineer who directed the building of the new Westminster bridge. He was first a member of Solomon's Temple Lodge, Hemmings Row (of which Desaguliers was Master), but later became Master of a lodge in Madrid, and is last mentioned as being Warden of the lodge at the White Bear in King's St, Golden Square, which is now the prestigious Royal Alpha Lodge No 16.

We should also note the Revd J. P. Stehlin, a member of the French lodge at the Swan, Long Acre, and also a Fellow of the Royal Society. He was a minister of several French churches from 1727 to his death in 1753 and, to emphasise the great contribution to a better learning of foreign languages introduced by Huguenots (who first used real sentences like *Où est la plume de ma tante?* to replace the dry recitation of declensions), we learn that this clergyman knew Hebrew, Greek, Latin, English, German, Italian, Danish, Dutch, Coptic, Armenian, Syriac, Arabic, Chaldee, Gothic, Old Tudesco and Anglo-Saxon, besides Spanish, Portuguese, Welsh and his native French.

In Canterbury we might notice the place of Thomas Roch, cabinet maker, who was a member of the first lodge there, that held at the Red Lion, and who was taken to court by the Carpenters for plying his trade without first applying for and obtaining the freedom of that city. And no less a furore was caused by the members of a lodge called *L'Immortalité de l'Ordre*, which was warranted on 16 June 1766 and only lasted nine years. After being constituted at the Crown and Anchor in the Strand, some by-laws were introduced which made the speaking of French compulsory in lodge and these were signed by one John de Vignoles, a relative of that distinguished Huguenot soldier, Major Francis La Balme Vignoles, who fought so bravely at Alicante in 1709 for a British cause.

This John De Vignoles signed himself 'Provincial Grand Master for Foreign Lodges' and later went on to exercise quite unauthorised power over new Masonic units in the area we now call Belgium. This was not the least of his misdemeanours and it should not therefore surprise us to learn that dissension was growing amongst the lodge members,

Leautier, Blache, Lapeyre and others, and not least when the famous (or infamous) Chevalier d'Eon was here made a Masonic member.

It can thus be seen that, like the well-known Masonic pavement, the involvement of Huguenot Masons in the Craft was not all sunshine and light. Nonetheless the benefits accruing to the Craft from the engagement of these brethren was, as in the nation as a whole, far more overweighted on the side of good than of any other quality. English life would never have been the same without the Huguenot touch (and I am one who loves oxtail soup). In no less a way, English Freemasonry stands beholden to many of that persuasion who graced its lodges.

Ainsi soit-il, as they used to say: So mote it be.

IS THERE ANYTHING MORE TO RESEARCH?

It was after I had been ordained a very short time that I experienced a crisis. I rang up an older and wiser clergyman and put my problem to him.

'As you know I am the assistant to a church with a large congregation and my Vicar expects me to preach at least once each week. I have been there six weeks and I have covered all the main points of the Christian Faith. I don't know what more to preach about. What am I to do? I can't admit to my Vicar that I have nothing more new to say.'

The older man was kind and helpful. 'Do you visit the parishioners?' he asked. 'Do you listen to the news on the radio or read the newspaper? Do you read your Bible regularly? Do you talk with your friends?'

I admitted that I did all those things.

'Then just begin to think about what you hear, read, see and talk about and let God do the rest,' was his advice.

I did and I have never stopped preaching from that day to this, 54 years on.

That in brief is the theme of my lecture to you today. It would be so easy to imagine that when you see all the books that have been written about Freemasonry, when you hear the lectures that have been given and note how many of them seem to repeat the subjects that you have heard, or heard of, before, and above all when you consider that the speculative Craft has been in existence for some 400 years and more, that everything that is of any consequence has already been researched to exhaustion. If that is what you may imagine to be the case then let me say that I too was once of that opinion. I too once wondered, as a new member of Quatuor Coronati Research Lodge, whatever new there could be to occupy my future years. That was 30 years ago. You will perhaps not be surprised to learn that, as with preaching, so with Masonic research, I have not only never stopped — I just wonder whether I will have enough time left to complete what I still have the desire to achieve.

How does such a change come about? Well, in much the same way as that by which my friend enabled me to effect a new approach to my preaching. It is done by looking afresh at the texts that I might think I am thoroughly familiar with, by reading the past and current journals of Freemasonry, by listening to what my friends and acquaintances are interested in knowing and not infrequently having them ask me to explain what nobody else has ever satisfactorily solved for them. Visiting new Masonic halls and seeing the artefacts they contain, or witnessing new forms of ritual or ceremony there, also helps — but reading the so-called 'authoritative' books and asking myself whether they really satisfy me is the greatest spur. Above all I know the truth of the saying, 'The more you know, the more you realise what you do not know.' When you find that even the sources that claim to have dealt with a topic themselves still leave gaps, then you know indeed that there is still more to research. Let us turn to some examples of what I mean.

Some fifteen years ago I was invited to give a first series of lectures in Australia and New Zealand. What the New Zealanders asked me to do was to produce something with a down-under flavour that had never been done before. They had lodge histories which told the story of how the first Freemasons set up their meetings in the colony and how those meetings developed into the oldest units that are extant in the country today. That was interesting and, as far as research in early New Zealand Masonry was concerned, there seemed to be nothing more that could be said. What no one had ever done, however, was to ask the questions: 'Where and what were the lodges in England, Ireland and Scotland from which those earliest Masonic pioneers emerged? Why was it those particular Masons who started the first lodges in their new world? What kind of Masonry did they bring with them and what influence did that English or other Masonry have on the emerging practices of Christchurch, Wellington or Auckland?'

In a field where everything seemed to have been said, a whole new gap appeared. I count it one of my real delights to have tried to begin to plug that hole and someone else one day will perhaps write an exhaustive survey of those first pioneers and their origins.

This recently led me on to enquire if anything of the same sort had ever been attempted for Canadian Freemasonry. Where did the first Freemasons on that continent come from and what traditions did they bring with them? Why did they set up the lodges in the places that they did and what links, if any, did they retain with the lodges back in Britain? What, for example, was the especial part played by the military personnel in this exercise and, since military lodges tended to be mainly of Irish or Scottish tradition in the early days, what effect did this have on the working and outlook of the first lodges there?

I feel myself already involved in this enterprise, because one of my recent commissions has been to research and then write up the story of the Cornwallis family, which began in 1230 and is still producing heirs to the line today. The Cornwallis family has been involved in English Freemasonry from at least 1725, when we know that a member of the family belonged to a lodge in London, but what is much more to our present purpose is the fact that no one has ever portrayed the whole story of this family's service to Masonry and this will be one of the matters that I include in my new biography. One of their sons was the Hon Edward Cornwallis, an officer in the 40th Regiment of Foot, which later became my own Lancashire Fusiliers, and in his service in Canada he formed the very first lodge in Halifax, Nova Scotia. I would like to think that in providing the full family history I shall be able to offer the descendants of that first lodge an even more complete background to their Founder.

Mention of the one Cornwallis leads on to another who made the surrender of the British forces at Yorktown in 1781. He too was not just an English General but also a regular Freemason. We know, for instance, that after his return to Britain Cornwallis provided Masonic charity for the children of General Benedict Arnold, who transferred his allegiance from the American to the British side. No one to my knowledge has ever pursued this matter though it might well be germane to another, as yet, unsolved mystery. What was the relationship, as Commanders, of those who were practising Freemasons whilst serving on opposite sides of the American War of Independence? Is there anything to confirm or disallow the thesis that certain strange and otherwise inexplicable military decisions might have been due to a strange reluctance of fellow-Freemasons to either engage in unnecessary slaughter or to press an advantage which would endanger their brother-opponent unduly? This raises the still larger question as to whether Masonic influence had anything to do with what we know generally to have been the strange courtesies of the 18th-century battlefield. Here again a whole new range of matters for research make their appearance.

On a visit to South Australia I noticed that the layout of many lodge items is almost exactly the reverse of what was common in the area around London, England, at the time that the pioneers first set up Masonic meeting places in this part of Australia. That puzzled me until, in one of the present halls in that area, I was told that the pictures of the earliest Past Masters were all produced the wrong way round because someone got the negative mixed up. That, I am sure, is what happened with a picture of an English lodge room. It was developed 'back to front' and hence much of the furniture was in the wrong place. Since the Grand Lodge there insists on uniformity, the mistake could have become the standard working style everywhere. New research, however, can have its unexpected revelations. We now know that certain northern English Freemasons imported these features.

Sitting down to read the not very well-thumbed pages of Masonic transactions produced by research lodges or Past Masters' associations can itself produce some very interesting material for reflection. It was by doing this with such publications in Manchester, Lancashire, ten years ago that I came up with what I believe is a refreshingly new area of study on how much operative Guild Masonry affected the later and more speculative Craft. Questions that had bemused me and others for a long time began at last to look like having new sorts of answers.

The whole field of early Craft and Royal Arch Masonry started to look like a more cohesive and natural whole, rather than a series of leaps and intrusions. What had hitherto seemed to be a closed shop of unlockable evidence began to reshape and to acquire a more natural and reasonable form. To use a true if well-worn metaphor, the pieces of the jigsaw started to fall into place and a more cohesive picture emerged. What is more, a different line of research opened up, producing evidence that affected not only the Craft but also the Royal Arch and the Mark degrees.

Having tackled the challenge to write a completely new book on the Mark and Royal Ark Mariner degrees, I had also to face the issue of what I could and could not accept in the previous books thought 'authoritative' on these matters. Time after time I have realised that previous efforts in this field have either not researched certain avenues enough or have come to conclusions that the evidence would not sustain.

When a Past Grand Secretary of our United Grand Lodge said to me with some disdain, 'Why ever do we need another book on those degrees?' I must confess that my heart took a skip. Perhaps he was right. Perhaps everything had been said on the subject and all that was needed was another reprint of the books by Grantham or Handfield-Jones. Yet something urged me on. I began to find that their treatments were incomplete, questions that I had asked of myself for years as a Provincial Grand Master in the degrees were not answered or answered satisfactorily. When one of them said that the Mark degree went through a thin and fitful time after 1813 and prior to its revival around 1850, I knew that something was wrong. In the event, I was able to write a whole chapter showing how the degree was fully alive and being practised at that period in every quarter of England, not to mention Scotland, Ireland and the USA, and that it was its vigour, and not its weakness, that led to the events from 1850 onwards. When the Grand Secretary of those degrees can say that the resulting account I have produced is a 'riveting read' and a 'scholarly survey' I know that new research has again paid off.

One of the side-effects of this latter work has been the support I have received from the Grand Chapter of Ireland. No one, they tell me, has so helpfully outlined the development of their degrees in the modern period and they are delighted that at last their manner of doing extra-Craft Masonry is properly related not only to their past but also to the sister Constitutions in the British Isles. What that sparked off in my mind immediately, as I prepared to come here, was the question: What was the contribution of Irish to Australian Freemasonry and has that field been adequately researched? I do not, you notice, ask whether the matter has been previously looked at but whether what has been written, if it has, has fully covered the subject. It might of course also link up with what I said earlier about discovering the origins of other Colonial Masonic founders.

Another line of research that was usefully opened up ten years ago in Quatuor Coronati Lodge could also be said to bear upon the whole matter of early Colonial Freemasonry. As an experiment we invited a non-Mason from Scotland to visit our lodge and deliver a lecture on 'Confessions of a Cowan: A Non-Mason and early Masonic History'.

The points which he made in the course of his paper were both refreshing and penetrating. He submitted three comments. First, that he was surprised on first discovering the amount, and the general quality, of work done in the historical field by Masonic researchers, and thought that it should be more widely known. Second, that what worried him in reading much of that work, at least in regard to Scotland, was the sense that, whilst what he read seemed sound in itself, it seemed to be written as if the rest of the society in which the events took place was quite dissociated from Freemasonry. And third, he realised that on the side of non-Masonic historians they had failed, especially in the realm of biography, to take any serious account of the fact that the characters they were dealing with as soldiers, sailors, politicians or entrepreneurs were also Freemasons. The severance of Freemasonry from its full social context was perhaps the greatest limitation on anyone producing really worthwhile research. He proposed that somehow or other a partnership between these two camps could not be other than beneficial, but how it could be best arranged he was not able at once to suggest.

If you think about the matter you may begin to see its implications in a number of ways. I have already hinted at one in my query about how or whether the commanders in the War of American Independence were swayed in their actions by being 'sons of the widow'. I wonder what difference it made that when Cornwallis returned from America, after what was considered publicly to be an ignominious surrender, he was made the King's Master General of the Ordnance — a major military appointment — and within seven years the virtual Governor of Ireland as the King's Lieutenant-Governor there. Did his being a Freemason have anything to do with that? If it did not, then did his being a Mason have anything to do with his highly successful tenure of the Irish post, so that even to this day it is thought that had he only been allowed to continue there, it is possible that the subsequent troubles in that land would have been largely avoided? That is something of what 'social Masonic research' can mean.

There is one even simpler field in which further research may be possible and this I commend to you with very great eagerness indeed. It starts with the ceremonies that we perform so regularly and which some of you are doubtless very proficient in performing. Yet do we fully understand what it is that we are saying or doing in these basic acts of Freemasonry? Do you, as I have to tell you that I still do, listen each time a ceremony happens and ask myself at some point or other whether I really know what was the origin, what is the significance, or what is the reason for a difference from elsewhere, of what I am seeing or hearing at that moment? Let me give you some examples:

When a candidate is being admitted to the lodge and is led blindfold to the Wardens, he is positioned so that he can strike the lodge officer on the shoulder. Why is that? And why in some lodges does the Warden leave his seat and stand in front of his pedestal in the path of the Deacon and candidate?

In the Second Degree there seems to be continuing debate, disagreement or disbelief concerning the place and purpose of the two great pillars said to have stood at the porchway (or) entrance of King Solomon's Temple. Just what is the solution to this puzzle and whatever are we to make of tracing boards that put them not at the entrance but at some side door of the holy edifice?

Still in the Second Degree, why do we claim that the staircase leading to the middle chamber had 15 or more steps and why do we say that it led from the south to the west in the temple whilst it goes north to east in our lodge rooms? Do you know what is behind this and where you could find an answer?

And finally in this short enquiry I turn to the opening ceremony of any District, Provincial or Grand Lodge and consider the answer given by the Junior Grand Warden to the question about his situation. He replies 'On Mount Tabor'. Why Mount Tabor that appears nowhere else in present-day Freemasonry? Why not Mount Moriah or Mount Zion? Where do we go to unravel any of these mysteries?

I have to tell you that I do not know of any standard textbook on Freemasonry that will straightforwardly answer these queries. If you are going to find the meaning or the origin of them you will have to do your own research — as I had to. Not that these are the only matters still to be unravelled.

Just before I came to Perth, Western Australia, I was presented with a new catalogue of the jewels that lie in the possession of the ancient York Lodge in the city of that name and of which, as a newcomer, I am but an honorary member. When the catalogue was presented to me by the compiler, he said this: 'I have listed every jewel in our possession. I have included every bit of information that I can obtain — but there are still 12 jewels that I am either uncertain about or completely uninformed. Would you kindly do what research you can and help me.'

The jewels have been there for 200 years and there is still research to be done on them.

Need I say anything more than this:

Si investigatio requiris, circumspice?